APOSTLE

and APOSTO

according
to the gospel of St. Matthew

LATE

by

Msgr. Lucien Cerfaux

Translated by

Donald D. Duggan
of the Louvain American College

DESCLEE COMPANY

NEW YORK — ROME — PARIS — TOURNAI   1960

NIHIL OBSTAT
THOMAS F. MALONEY
Censor Deputatus

IMPRIMATUR July 8, 1959
✠ PATRICK A. O'BOYLE
ARCHBISHOP OF WASHINGTON

LIBRARY OF CONGRESS CATALOG CARD NUMBER : 60-6515

This is a translation from DISCOURS DE MISSION (Desclée & Cie,
Tournai, Belgium, 1956)

CONTENTS

v

Introduction

Jesus once composed a set of instructions for his missionaries, both present and future. This shall be the subject of our meditation, as it is preserved for us in the Gospels, and especially in St. Matthew's Gospel 9: 35 to 10: 42.

Yet this advice was given for only a small mission in Galilee, a trip of a few weeks in the villages of one province. " Do not go among the Gentiles, and do not enter the cities of the Samaritans. Go rather to the lost sheep of the house of Israel, and as you go, preach this message: ' The Kingdom of Heaven is at hand! ' " (*Matt.* 10: 5-7)

Does it matter in the history of the world what a few peasants might say to each other in such a backward corner of the world? Yes! for this was the foundation of the Church, the model of all its missions: the starting point, the nucleus and seed of all that would later develop.

God has a habit of doing great things with nothing. He loves to create.

The saints understood this and they accomplished great works with nothing at all, like God, because in their work they followed His methods. The anchorites of the desert spent their lives battling against the evil spirits. St. Benedict, driven from Subiaco, founded only the monastery of Monte Cassino. St. Francis of Assisi formed but a few dozen disciples as guardians of his thought. The Curé of Ars heard confessions in a village church. But it is these humble works which shine. When the apostolate is thus understood, it weighs heavily in the balance of God and the spiritual destiny of the world.

Do you think the noisy apostolate will count for much in the history of the Church? No apostolate, no work, will ever re-echo like the obscure mission of Galilee. And yet what was it in square miles? Galilee is no larger than an American county.

It is neither the surface nor the length nor the width that counts. It is the depth. The apostolate is measured by the plumb line, not the tape measure. " Jesus chose the twelve that they might be always with him, and that he might send them out to preach. " (*Mark* 3: 14)

An apostle is truly an apostle only when he remains united to our Lord. Contemplation and action should not be separated. Mary and Martha are sisters. The two sisters complement each other and make only one. That is how the saints understood it.

For with the saints, too, the apostolate and the interior life are one and the same thing. The holy Curé of Ars could hardly find time to say his prayers, but what a prayer was his life! St. Francis hesitated his whole life long between the solitude of a hermitage and the work of preaching. St. Benedict Labre was an apostle by his prayers.

The apostolate is just the glow of sanctity. Apostoles should be doubly holy, once for themselves, and once for others.

Just as the mission of the Apostles is the mission pattern which will be reproduced countless times until the very end of time, so the advice of our Lord is our pattern too. It is true for all missions and for all apostolates.

Our Lord gave his Apostles simple, fundamental rules. It is up to us to apply them to
our own more complicated lives.

Surely we need the Holy Spirit to
understand deeply. And the Holy Spirit comes
to us only by prayer; He speaks to us *only
in silence.*

These pages have one ambition: to nourish
with the word of the Gospel the beginnings
of all those projects, methods and activities
which are consecrated to the Kingdom of God.

Part one

THE MISSION

And Jesus went about all the cities, and towns, teaching in their synagogues, and preaching the gospel of the Kingdom, and healing every disease, and every infirmity. Seeing the crowd, he had pity on them: for they were bewildered and dejected, like sheep without a shepherd. Then he said to his disciples: The harvest indeed is great, but the laborers are few. Pray the Lord of the harvest to send laborers into his harvest.

And having called his twelve disciples together, he gave them power over unclean spirits, to cast them out, and to heal all manner of diseases, and all manner of infirmities. And the names of the twelve apostles are these: The first, Simon who is called Peter, and Andrew his brother. James the son of Zebedee, and John his brother, Philip and Bartholomew, Thomas and Matthew the publican, and James the son of Alpheus, and Thaddeus. Simon, the Cananean, and Judas Iscariot, who also betrayed him. These twelve Jesus sent: commanding them, saying: Do not go among the Gentiles, and do not enter the cities of the Samaritans. Go rather to the lost sheep of the house of Israel. And as you go, preach this message: The Kingdom of Heaven is at hand. Heal the sick, raise the dead, cleanse the lepers, cast out devils: freely have you received, freely give. Do not try to gather together, for your journey, either gold or silver, or even any small change in your sashes. Do not take a wallet for the road; nor two tunics, nor shoes, nor staff: the laborer is worthy of his hire. When you come to a town or a village, find out if there is a respectable house and stay there until you leave the city. And when you come into the house, salute it, saying: Peace be to this house. And if that house is worthy, your peace will come upon it; but if it is not worthy, your peace will return to you. And wherever they will not receive you or listen to your words, shake off the dust from your feet as you leave that city or that house. Amen I say to you, it will be more tolerable for the land of Sodom and Gomorrha in the day of judgment than for that city.

Matthew 9: 35 - 10: 15

I

Lost sheep

" Go rather to the lost sheep of the house of Israel. " (Matt. 10: 6)

Lost sheep ... The apostolate begins with a great pity, the pity of God. God has pity on His creatures who damn themselves.

Recall the good shepherd, who leaves his ninety-nine sheep in the desert and goes in search of the one which is lost. He returns carrying it on his shoulders.

The good shepherd is God; and it is our Lord who takes his place. He is the Father of the prodigal son, the one whom the lost child called from the sleepless depth of his fever and misery, " I will arise and go to my Father. " The Father knows that His son is suffering; He is suffering with him. No matter that it is the prodigal's own fault and that the Father has been offended. The child is suffering. That is enough for the Father's pity. And besides, it is He who gave man the liberty he has abused. God does not will the loss of His creatures; He would save man in spite of himself, if that were possible. Here is the mystery: that man could abuse his liberty.

There were many lost sheep of the house of Israel in the time of our Lord. There always are. And here is another mystery: the abuse of the liberty given by God. Just as we are saved together in the Church, so we damn ourselves together. Certain ages are evil. They seem to form a secret pact between the weakness of souls and the exterior temptations which lie in wait about them. They raise up evil shepherds who, instead of protecting their flock, ravage it.

The evil shepherds of our Lord's time have a name. They are the Chief Priests and the Pharisees. The Priests did their job at the temple of Jerusalem, but we dare not say they did it honestly. Their office filled their pockets, so that they lived like rich men, like the Greeks; in other words, like pagans. The thought never occurred to them that these folk, whose first fruits and tithes and sacrificial victims they accepted, had souls to save. The Pharisees thought about souls, but only about their own and their disciples': the privileged souls. They despised the humble and the souls of the humble, " lost sheep of the house of Israel. "

Only Jesus thought of the humble. But how he thought of them! All his life they were his sorrow: " Seeing the crowd, he had pity on them: for they were bewildered and dejected, like sheep without a shepherd. " (*Matt.* 9: 36). This very pity was the cause of his death, for he discredited himself in the eyes of the Pharisees and the Priests by mingling with the poor, with " sinners, " and by preaching to them that the Kingdom of God had been made for them, too—and for them above all. Such an attitude condemned the leaders, and they had their vengeance. Jesus carried his cross on the shoulders which had borne the lost sheep.

The Master has scarcely uttered this word of pity when a prophetic vision rises before his eyes. This whole unhappy people is the Father's harvest. ⟨ God did not create it for the eternal fire, but to gather up the good grain into the barns, " the harvest is plentiful. " (*Matt.* 9: 37⟩

Jesus is working at the harvest. Until now he has worked alone. His preaching (such as the sermon on the Mount) has aroused souls. His word has fallen on the ground, and when it met good ground it sprung up, for it is the seed of God. It ripened and gave God sheaves heavy with grain.

⟨ But Jesus is not to work alone. He is going to gather helpers, for he tells them,

" The harvest indeed is great, but the laborers are few. " Workers are needed. " Pray the Lord of the harvest to send laborers into his harvest. " (*Matt*. 9: 38). God, the Master, chooses the workers, sends them out and gives them their orders.)

The Apostles are thus born of prayer, their own prayer and their own desire. Is it not always thus? In prayer God reveals what He expects of us. The purity and the intensity of our prayer measure the greatness of God's demands. If Benedict Labre had not suffered and prayed so much, he would not have known the will of God for him. All the saints are " Orantes, " " prayer made man " as Thomas of Celano said of St. Francis of Assisi. Of that prayer the apostolate is born and nourished.

Every vocation to the apostolate begins with a vision of souls. There are lost sheep, a harvest to gather. The saints could only repeat these ideas from century to century. Can we do better than to open our eyes to the awesome vision of the miseries and the possibilities of salvation offered by our times, which are probably no better or worse than other times . . .?

Sheep without shepherds. Let us reflect on this. Since the apostolate whose preoccupations are most like those of the primitive church is the parish, let us imagine a modern pastor arriving in his parish.

He has made his first visit. Now he knows what has become of the grace of baptism in these souls, in a parish of the twentieth Christian century, in our Christian lands, where the Virgin is honored and the Blessed Sacrament carried in procession. If the pastor were a saint, here is what he might say to his parishioners in his first Sunday sermon. " Christ wept over Jerusalem, and I weep over you . . . How could I keep from weeping, my brothers? Hell exists. I didn't invent it; God has told us. You don't think about it, and what you do will take you there. " I did not have to invent this sermon. It is the first one Father Vianney made to his parishoners at Ars. Vianney was a saint, or was to become one. To talk thus of sin and hell, one must be holy; one must " feel " what it is for a soul to damn itself.

What good is it to describe our times in detail? We know well enough the dangerous path by which we are being driven in an effort to be considered modern. The ease of life, the noise which dazes, the images of the movies, the propaganda of ideas: all these are forces reducing the intelligence to the state of a machine and destroying all reflection and will.

Once the shepherdess knitted as she watched her sheep, and took the time to become holy. Now—if there are any shepherdesses left—she reads a paperback novel and dreams the sensual images absorbed in the movie theater. Noise smothers the silence of God. The world's pandemonium has an orchestra leader, for the retreat toward the material away from the spiritual is continual. We are going logically toward the very obvious end of dechristianization, the " denaturalization " of our race. The orchestra leader could well be he who is ever opposed to Christ, the " enemy " of Gospel parable. There we have a situation tragic for religion in contemporary society.

" You blaspheme the name of God, " said the holy pastor of Ars, continuing his sermon. " You spend your nights in the taverns. You give yourself over to the evil pleasures of the dance. You plunder your neighbor's field. You do many things to offend God. Do you think that God does not see you? He sees you, as I see you, my children, and you will be treated as you deserve. "

Happy times, when the pastor only had these peccadillos to reprimand, trifles, the sins of a people who still have the faith. Today no one commits those sins—they are not worth the trouble. Now we live an abstract sin: materialism and the denial of the super-natural.

Harvests to gather. Man can never quite smother his soul. He is so made that his gross pleasures satiate him without appeasing his desires. The prophets ceaselessly reveal the soul to itself and repeat the ancient words of Amos: " There is a hunger in the land, not a hunger for bread, and not a thirst for water, but for the sound of the words of God. " (*Amos* 8: 11) " Not by bread alone does man live, but by every word that comes from the mouth of God. " (*Matt.* 4: 4)

Because we love God, we must come closer to our brother men, to understand them. " Show me, if you can, an idle love, " says St. Augustine.

St. Theresa of the Child Jesus realized her vocation on the day when, before the cross, she felt her heart sink at the thought of all the souls for whom Christ suffered in vain. " Since that day, the dying cry of Jesus, ' I thirst ' has continually re-echoed in my heart, lighting there a hidden but very living flame. I wanted to give my beloved to drink. I, too, thirsted for souls, and I desired at any cost to snatch sinners from the eternal flames. "

Our pity, our works, our charity bring us *into the world* where the lost sheep are wandering. We must know the world. For that one need not be " of the world. " The best way to know a river is not to drift down it like a lifeless piece of wood, but to have a light, solid boat with a good motor; to be master of the currents and to go in the direction we wish, even (and especially) " against the current. "

For great evils need great remedies. God is asking us to be something purely supernatural in the world. Satiated and unsatisfied, the world is awaiting this of us, too. What will happen to our generation we do not know. One thing we do know, that we are preparing the future, the future of God.

2

The choice

Who are these Twelve, the " elect " of our Lord, his disciples *par excellence?*

Why this unequalled privilege: " You shall sit upon twelve thrones to judge the twelve tribes of Israel? " (*Matt.* 19: 28)

" He called to him men of his own choosing, " says St. Mark (3: 13). That is the profound reason for every vocation. We count for nothing. What proportion could there be between a human life, purely natural, and a divine task, even if humanly speaking the instrument had some value? And God often does without human preparations and human talents completely.

Here we have an enterprise of " God and Company. " God is the manager of the business. He is the one who makes the investments.

There was once a priest who did not know enough moral theology to receive the faculties of confessor from his bishop. The major seminary did not want to keep him. Yet this unlearned man was to be so " enlightened " by God that a hundred years ago all France, and the whole world, flocked to his confessional. God does not pay any attention to human estimates.

Now before choosing his Apostles, our Lord went up the mountain to pray. He called down the Holy Spirit on his work. Was that not to see who among his disciples were worthy to become his Apostles? No. He called whomever he wished. If he made his choice in the light of the Spirit, it is in order that this light might fall upon the Apostles, illuminating and transforming them. By being chosen they became worthy of the choice.

The divine choice, then, supposes no superiority or excellence. Rather, it gives the man everything he lacks.

If he could let himself forget the heavenly glory of the Apostles, St. Francis would give us another reason for their choice. " Our Lord, " he would say, " has found nothing more unworthy upon the earth. " That was his answer when Brother Bernard de Quintavalle asked him, " Why you? Why you? "

The divine choice supposes above all the *nothingness* of the creature. Assent by the creature can only mean total acceptance of God.

The apostolate thus rests on a humiliation. First came that of our Lord. Who was more humble than he? Who knew as he did the nothingness of the creature? Who knew better than he who bore our sins what sin adds to this nothingness? Based on the supreme humiliation of the Incarnation of the Word of God, the whole work of salvation is thus based on humility. Humility is its mark. This is the thesis of Von Ruville in " The Mark of the True Ring ": humility is the sign of the true religion and the true Church. " It was by an act of humble obedience that the work of salvation began. . . . " Remember the Magnificat and the crib.

For the choice of the first Apostles, then, the choice of the Twelve, our Lord applies a divine rule. And perhaps never again would a choice be so unexpected. " Who would dream of such mad impudence, except the Omnipotent, to give to such the task of conquering the world? " (Sertillanges). Our Lord chose the humble, then; not only humiliated, but truly humble, the " least. "

We would not want him to have chosen the great ones, Herod or Pilate, the Chief Priests or the Pharisees. A native instinct makes us prefer the Apostles, who had only their fishing boat and their simplicity.

The same divine policy continues and will continue. Listen to St. Paul speaking to the Corinthians of their Christian vocation. " There are not many wise, or rich, or noble among us. But God has chosen all that is least, and what is not, to put to shame the wise and the powerful. " (*I Cor*. 1: 26-27). St. Paul calls this policy the wisdom of God.

Then come the " least " of St. Francis, humble and last. With them the Gospel, the work of God, will begin again.

The holy Curé of Ars saw things in the same light. " Certainly, " he said, " many people come to consult me. But why? Just take a look at me. Because I am and I always will be the last priest of the diocese. " When his jealous brother priests wrote to the bishop, he joined with them to obtain his disgrace. Later he told, " I was waiting from one moment to the next to be driven away with clubs, convicted and condemned to end my days in prison. It seemed to me that everyone should have been against me for having dared to stay so long in a parish where I could only be an obstacle to good. "

It is striking that the saints believed what they said. And even more striking still is the fact that it is *true*. They are the humblest of all, because they understand better than all others the wisdom of God and the nothingness of the creature.

Only one condition is required of these would-be apostles. They must abandon the little they possess, their ship; their father and brothers, their house and their concerns, their occupation, their money, and their books if they had any. "We have left all to follow you." The only concern that Jesus asks of them is the preparation of humility and renunciation, annihilation.

We also make our renunciation, and it is a pledge of benediction, provided that we do not make of it a merit, a gift that we offer to God. We are so clever at stepping into the limelight, letting God know of His obligations.

This is certainly the doctrine of our Lord and the saints.

Now all this seems like a paradox. Are we not bound to serve God with our natural talents? And thus to cultivate them to the maximum? Is that not the apostolate, to put one's natural gifts and all one's activities in the service of his neighbor?

The magazine "La Vie Spirituelle" (February, 1946) asked, "Towards what type of sanctity are we moving?" Many answers considered sanctity as the utmost realization of human nature. "I do not approve of St. John of the Cross ... because his sanctity is inhuman. For him one became a saint despite his nature, erasing every human trait. But for me sanctity comes through nature —by perfecting one's natural gifts to the highest degree. The sanctity of St. John of the Cross seems to me to go against the parable of the talents. " (p. 238; cf. p. 232 ff.)

These principles are applied thus to the apostolate: " Until now the apostolate consisted in the sacrifice of one's natural gifts. But we carry on the apostolate by perfecting these gifts. You cite saints to us. We will cite others: St. Augustine and St. Thomas Aquinas, both geniuses who put their natural gifts, the talents of the parable, into the service of God. "

The parable of the talents should not deceive us. The talents which the servants receive from their master as he leaves on a long trip are not human qualities or human " talents, " as would imply an exegesis which forgets the lessons of the Fathers. These talents are God's graces, which pass through the hands of the apostle. There is no proportion between natural gifts and the supernatural gift of a mission. The apostle, lost in his work, is a creature apart; and there is no path leading from natural virtue to the exercise of sanctity. " There is space for the rivers of the world to roar comfortably between the most gigantic virtue and a most rudimentary sanctity. " (Léon Bloy)

It is another order. To use natural talents, they must be transformed ... crushed at the foot of the crucifix, in one way or another. They must again become gifts of God, supernatural, and perceived by us as such.

Thus God works in ways that are strange to us. Sometimes He gives *His gifts* while seeming to take our natural gifts into account. He made St. Augustine a genius of religious thought, and raised an intelligence already open to virtue to the heights of contemplation.

But at other times he makes Curés of Ars! And he prefers this latter policy.

One day on a pilgrimage to Ars, Lacordaire, the great orator of Notre Dame, agreed to speak in the pulpit of the holy Curé. On that day the listeners went home disappointed. They had not come to hear an orator, but a saint. They were not mistaken there. And neither is God mistaken. He prefers to give his graces to sanctity.

Concretely, then, how should we act?

We must use our natural gifts, but remain conscious of the place they hold. We must put them in their true place. They are not even a drop in the ocean of the grace of God.

Let us work with our natural talents, but especially with prayer and the grace which it merits.

Here is the opinion of a nun, " Works, as they are usually performed, deceive us, They do not seem to me to touch the soul. Instead, they often remain on the human plane, and go no deeper. " And another: " Catholic action, it seems to me, has other aims than sanctity. I find that our times put too much accent on the apostolate conceived as a direct action on others. It remains external, and too often has no real soul. "

We are faced with a crisis, the crisis of activity. We do too much. We do not reflect enough, we do not pray enough. We give, and often we have nothing to give. The true apostolate is to give of one's own holiness.

Of course, if we had to wait to attain sanctity before we could act, nothing would be done. But we must act with the beginnings of sanctity which are within us, mindful that this ounce of sanctity is what counts.

Our Lord sent his Apostles before they were saints. But the counsels he gave them, as we shall see, aimed at making them saints. And it was the apostolate which sanctified them.

This is the way we should be apostles. Our apostolate is on the right track if it sanctifies us, if it unites us to God. It is wrong if it separates us from God, empties us of grace and dissipates us. The secret is to be sent *and yet remain with Jesus*.

3

Apostolic travelers

St. Rock, patron of tramps, pray for us.

Here we have some very *practical* advice. Let us see the mission concretely. " Do not try to gather together, for your journey, either gold or silver, or even any small change in your sashes (the sash was used as a purse). Do not take a wallet for the road (no provisions); nor two tunics, nor shoes, nor staff (you will find food along the way): the laborer is worthy of his hire. " (*Matt.* 10: 9-10)

Our Lord knew his Apostles well. Prudent, careful, like all peasants, and Jews on top of it all. When they got into the ship with our Lord, they were careful to take on bread for the trip. If Jesus had let him, Matthew, the former publican, would surely have found funds amongst his old friends to finance the trip. They would have taken

33

at least one extra tunic, a sturdy traveler's sack, a handy staff, and good shoes for the long marches.

We hesitate to get rid of the staff, for although it can serve as a protection against thieves, still it marks one as a traveler. The evangelists did not know either whether to permit it or forbid it. Nor did our saints, those exegetes whom we have chosen as guides. When St. Francis heard these words, he threw down the staff he held in his hand. St. Benedict Labre, in the last weeks of his life, asked his Roman host for a stronger staff, since the one he possessed did not support the weight of his wretched body.

What counts is to penetrate the profound thought of our Lord. These short, practical counsels suggest *an attitude*. The Apostles must set out without scrip, without shoes, *without precautions*, for only thus will they enter into the state of soul desired by our Lord.

Our Lord does not want his Apostles, the apostolic travelers, to be well insured against all risks. Just the opposite: he desires the risk, because the risk makes them count on the Providence of God. Risks put holes in the web of life, and it is Providence which fills these holes.

Our civilization has renounced risk, and at the same time, Providence. " Our epoch, " writes Thibon, " seems to be placed completely under the sign of insurance. Ultimately there would be no more hazards, no more dangers. Everything will be foreseen, regulated, guaranteed. No one will risk anything any more. The myth of absolute and universal insurance is summed up in this terrible slogan: " Foresight which does away with Providence. "

But our Lord puts us under the hand of Providence. If all Christians should count on God, how much more his apostolic travelers! We must get used to living like children of our Heavenly Father, depending directly on him, responsible to him as to our immediate superior. We owe him everything. We should give all to him, and expect all from him.

Concrete, immediate confidence in Providence is like the fringe on the cloak of hope. For a prosaic epoch like ours, with neither force nor enthusiasm, it is difficult to rise on the wings of hope! We, the apostles, ought to do just that.

To travel as we have just described, with only one tunic, poor shoes for our feet, and no provisions for tomorrow, is to travel like the poor. Only the poor go on foot, exposed to circumstances, to all the dangers of the road, to hunger and thirst and nakedness, to shipwreck and discomfort.

Here *poverty* is introduced into our life.

The poor man has no savings. He has no stocks and bonds. He has no insurance policies, nor does he need any. The poor man lives from day to day, and thus can turn his face towards the Kingdom of Heaven.

Thus, for the journey of the Apostles, our Lord applied the principle of poverty understood as a religious virtue.

St. Francis accented poverty. Certainly he was a traveler, a pilgrim to foreign lands, but he fell in love with poverty. He loved it because it had been the companion of our Lord and our Lady, and was deserted. He loved it because of the profound detachment it brings about in our lives.

He loved it for its apostolic value. " The servant of God should ask alms more joyfully than if he were traveling about scattering coins to the winds. " In exchange for alms, the Poverillo gives his benefactor a priceless spiritual treasure.

In the modern world our poverty is a living sermon, proclaiming the primacy of the spiritual. Let us take care to preserve it in its integrity. Jordan has drawn a cruel caricature of false poverty and the false Franciscan in writing of Salimbene, a very early Franciscan. " It is amusing, for example, to compare the great pleasure Salimbene takes in professing absolute poverty, with the completely mediocre idea he has of that poverty. He considers it a special title to temporal favors from Providence, and a claim on the riches of others. It consists in possessing nothing, but receiving much, and if the world acted as it should, the Friars Minor would be living suitably and decently, with an abundance of the necessities of life. Seen in this light, with all the little defects which he is not careful to correct—love of comfort and good food, laziness and curiosity, a taste for gossip and the off-color story, he shows us the picture of a man who is very attached to the little things of this world, after having renounced the more important ones by his state in life. "

In the mind of our Lord and the saints there is also, I think, a certain mistrust of the conveniences which civilization puts at our disposal, even to the extent of apparently cutting down the efficiency of the Apostles.

With good shoes the Apostles could have visited more villages ... But the most important thing is sanctity.

We must understand this *protest against material civilization*. Bound to riches, civilization finds itself, like them, under the sign of Satan. Remember the third temptation:

Satan promises to give our Lord the kingdoms of the earth, with all their glory (that is, their riches) "*si cadens adoraveris me*, if you will recognize me as your master."

Lady Poverty, the spouse of our Lord whom St. Francis took in, is really much older than the gospel story. Abraham had already met her on his path when he received his vocation: "Go, leave your country and your father's house, and come into the land I will show you." The country of Abraham, Ur, in Chaldea, was a city in an ancient sedentary civilization where life was quite comfortable. The patriarch condemned himself to a nomadic life, with all the austerity and spiritual riches implied.

In the "Voyage of the Centurion" Psichari tells how one day he proudly showed the Moorish nomads some radio towers and a broadcasting station installed by the French. "Do you think that there is any other power on earth like ours?" he said. Sidia, his young guide, answered, "Truly, you French have the kingdom of earth; but we Moors have the kingdom of heaven."

Throughout the history of the Old Testament the graces destined for the chosen people seem to depend on their rejection of civilization. "I will lead her into the desert," says God by the lips of Osee, "and I will speak to her heart, and it will be as in the days of the flight from Egypt (when Israel was still nomadic. ") (*Osee* 2: 16-17)

We must pray to know in what measure to use human means in the apostolate. After a period of infatuation, a new direction is indicated. We feel that we are almost defeated on this battlefield. That is the sign that God demands something else: absolute confidence in supernatural methods, grace, the sacraments and his Word. Material civilization, all the skill which we see rising so proudly out of the dead souls of men, cannot reconcile us with civilization as it is.

If we want to be apostles, let us hold on to our Lord's principles. It is not a question of exhausting every natural means seeking all the possibilities of press or film. The best apostle will always be the saint. And the saint will always have the temptation to imitate Christ and the saints to the letter.

4

" Greet no one "

" And greet no one along the way. "

(Luke 10: 4)

Just a word of advice, apparently of little importance, even seeming to go against common politeness ... Again we must look for more profound intentions in Our Lord's words.

The Apostles carry a message which should arrive at its destination as quickly as possible, without any loss or dissipation along the way. They must run, pressing to their hearts the peace which is their burden. To stop along the road, utter idle words, is to bungle the divine message.

The Apostles, like all Orientals, like to spend time in long greetings, which we call today salaams (an Arab greeting meaning "peace be with you"). Salaams are for the leisure class, for worldly visits, and for tea parties.

But the Apostles should become *men in a hurry*, in a hurry for God. They do not have time to amuse themselves along the way. " Amen, I say to you, you will not have traveled through all the cities of Israel before the Son of Man comes. " (*Matt.* 10: 23). That is why they must hurry; God's time is short.

We who do the work of God must also hurry, for the time is short. St. Paul was ever a man in a hurry, always busy running from one city to the next, rarely stopping, pressed that the Gospel might enter every town with him. And we carry with us the grace of God.

Is not the apostolate a harvest? Harvesters are always in a hurry, ever fearful of the threatening storm. The work of God is marked with our apostolic haste, for on it depends the salvation of a definite number of souls. This was true even for the little mission of the Apostles in Galilee. Grace was passing among the men of Galilee during those days, and the fact that the Apostles ran faster or slower decided the eternal destiny of a certain number of Galileans.

And so our Lord wants the Apostles to consider themselves as very busy men, very businesslike, but about their own business. One day he will reproach them in a parable for not having as much skill in spiritual affairs as the men of the world, who have a temporal occupation, have for their own business. These are more zealous and more skillful than the children of light in their spiritual affairs.

Do you realize the kind of inhuman life led by certain financiers and industrialists who are caught up in their businesses? How much patience, sleeplessness and austerity scholars need to accomplish their mission?

Our Lord wants the Apostles to have the physical sensation of being in a hurry. That is why he forbad them any greetings. The Apostles obeyed blindly. They do not make distinctions when our Lord tells them something. Thus our Lord accustomed them to carrying out their apostolic labor in haste, with the conviction that they have a heavy responsibility.

Perhaps they did not fully understand, just now, the importance of their task. Later, after Pentecost, they would understand it better.

I think that our Lord had still another intention. The Apostles left two by two. If they talk to no one along the way, they will have soon confided in each other. And then, in deep silence, they will have a more profound conversation in that house of God which is the soul. We are always speaking to someone. In silence, we speak to God.

The Apostles are to *pray as they travel*. That is what our Lord wanted to teach them. They say the only prayer they know, the one which our Lord taught them: the " Our Father. "

What beautiful " Our Fathers " the Apostles must have recited as they traversed the harvests of Galilee. Thy kingdom come! In prayer their mission received its true meaning. Thy kingdom come! These Apostles were the founders of this kingdom; at their prayer and at their word heaven came down to earth, and devils fled in terror.

When the disciples return from their apostolic tour full of enthusiasm, they will tell our Lord: " The devils fled before us! " " Yes, " answers our Lord, " I saw the conquest of the kingdom of Satan; but do not rejoice so much at that. The true reason for your joy is that your names are written in heaven. " (*Luke* 10: 18, 20)

The Apostles are the first to benefit from the Kingdom of God. How could it be otherwise? Those who established the Kingdom establish it first in themselves.

According to God's principles an Apostle, because he is an Apostle, is saved, chosen, already established in heaven. In the measure in which we share in the mission of the Apostles worthily, we are already saved. Our salvation is measured by our gift of self to our apostolic vocation, which includes our salvation.

Thus we may forget about our personal salvation and center our life on this one desire: that the Kingdom of God be established fully, that it take in all men, ourselves included. By our apostolic work and our cooperation with God our names are written in heaven.

The apostolic mission continues, always the task of men in a hurry, completely occupied by the Kingdom of God. Our task is to save souls, and the most souls possible. " The Kingdom of Heaven is like the head of a household who goes out early in the morning to hire workers for his vineyard. " (*Matt.* 20: 1) He keeps on hiring them until the eleventh hour.

Thus God continues to hire apostolic workers, first the Twelve, then the seventy-two. After Pentecost came the great horde of workers in the vineyard: St. Peter, St. Paul, the whole history of the Church. God will hire workers for his vineyard forever, until the end of time.

We are the hired hands, and it is the great joy of our lives. People are unhappy because they have no task to take up their attention. They search ceaselessly, and ever end face to face with themselves, terrified at their own mediocrity.

Our vocation is to work in the Kingdom of God, and such is our mission. There are so many troubles in the world! There are physical troubles—which some day may be overcome. But moral troubles—who bothers about that? Disorientated lives, lack of ideals, deliberate denial of all ideals, the dreadful absence of God—who cares about that?

It is our job. We must not wait for someone else to do it.

We are beginning the mission of the Apostles all over again, as if nothing had ever been done. But in the Kingdom of God one can never say that nothing has been done.

Let us obey our Lord to the letter. Let us not stop, not greet any one along the way.

Let us not listen to the voices which want to slow us down, the doubts which weaken our enthusiasm for the labor of an apostle. "Haven't I abused God's graces? Am I worthy of this mission? Will I have the courage I need? I've made so many resolutions, and I always fail."

There is always time to begin again and again.

We should not be discouraged if for half a lifetime we have not been fully faithful. If we only have five minutes left, it is for those five minutes that God has chosen us, for one last moment.

Or perhaps the evil voices whisper within us: " We have carried the brunt of the day's heat. We are dying of fatigue from an apostle's work, and meanwhile everyone else is enjoying the happiness of the life we have refused. " Experience proves that this is a fallacious argument. Those who are detached are much happier than those who seek their own happiness in life's ordinary joys. It is easier to be happy in austerity than amid the pleasures of this life. Sometimes, of course, the human machine cries out. Let it pass. Let us not stop for the petty consolation of self love, of human cares and human affections. Let us give ourselves completely.

Let us keep silence. It would seem that our Lord spoke for our times. Silence was never so useful as it is today, for never has the world made so much noise.

Just consider that we have the movies, radio, television, the papers, all those voices coming at us from every spot on the globe, voices of politicians and comedians and sports commentators. . . .

An apostle, then, should resolutely take up his abode in solitude and silence, that silence in which the tremendous voice of the Holy Spirit makes itself heard to pray with us.

49

" *Spiritus Domini replevit orbem terrarum.* "
The sound of the Holy Spirit re-echoes across
the earth, and the world makes much noise
to avoid hearing it.

Let us sum it all up in the word *solitude*.

The more the modern world is full of
noise and agitation, too many contacts,
exaggerated depersonalization, the more the
apostle should know that only his solitude
lets him identify himself with his Creator and
Master (how many inventions there are to
rob man of his solitude, of his very self!).

Jesus sought the solitude of the mountains
at nightfall. The Twelve cultivated this
solitude on their apostolic journeys. St. Paul
grew in silence, as did the anchorites of the
desert. Silence reigned in the monasteries of
St. Benedict of Nurcie. St. Francis of Assisi
demanded silence in the Portiuncula. St. Benedict Labre kept a most mysterious silence,
like a hermit, unknown, refusing to give his
address to his own and hiding even his name.
" A saint is a creature so much apart, so
cloistered, so tremendously silent, that one
might take him for a kind of living plant in
the lost Paradise. " (Léon Bloy)

In the solitude of prayer and compliance
God takes possession of the apostolic soul.
If our works are to have eternal value they
must come from the depths, from where the

Kingdom of Heaven meets the nothingness that we are. Extremes often meet, and there is a mysterious link between the heights of God and the depths of man.

If man searches in the depth of his soul, and stays there, he finds God. Solitude and silence bring us to bedrock. Then our works are eternal works. Otherwise they are only exterior agitation, with no effect on the Kingdom of God. We may be sure that God is not going to reward all the works of our generation, but those founded on silence, austerity, renunciation, and poverty.

5

Villages and houses

There are some risks which should not be taken. " When you come to a town or a village, find out if there is a respectable house and stay there until you leave the city. " (*Matt*. 10: 11). Travelers who come to a strange city inquire beforehand to find a suitable hotel. The Apostles should act likewise. It is touching to see our Lord come down to such concrete advice.

Let us be prudent. Let us seek persons of our side, houses worthy of the Kingdom of God.

We should not forget that here below we are on foreign soil, citizens of another country, exiles like Abraham, of whom the Scripture says, " By faith Abraham obeyed the voice of God, to set out for the land which he should receive for an inheritance, although he did leave without knowing where he was going. By faith he lived like a stranger, dwelling in tents, with Isaac and Jacob, who were co-heirs in the promise: he was searching for a city with firm foundations, whose architect and whose builder is God. " (*Heb.* 11: 8-10)

We should not naively believe that everyone thinks like we do and that every house is worthy to receive us. This is not a question of pride, but of prudence.

When the Apostles have chosen a house they are not to leave it for another. " Stay there until you leave the city. " (*Matt.* 10: 11)

Oriental hospitality is proverbial. Every guest is sent by God; when he comes there is a feast, and the first meal is lavish. But supplies are quickly used up ... or else generosity wearies. The travelers might be tempted to change houses so that the feast can begin again a little farther down the road.

The Apostles are to have none of this paltriness. That is the natural way to act, as men in the world act when they are seeking their own advantage or comfort. It is enough for the Apostles to find a " worthy " and respectable house. The rest does not count. For travelers who do not even have the right to have a change of tunic and shoes on their feet, what difference does it make if they are comfortable or not?

All this does not seem quite so petty when we look again at the attitude which our Lord is trying to implant. The worker of the Gospel must sacrifice everything for his mission, gaging everything by the Kingdom of God. He accepts his relations with the world inasmuch as they help him spread his message. He does not seek these relations for themselves. He does not stop to enjoy them. He is detached from everything which is not the task before him. We are used to our Lord's manner now: if the Apostles keep an obvious rule in this case they will be taking an attitude of detachment, and this attitude will become habitual.

There is a test of our value as an apostle in our behavior with the world. That is how tradition understood it. In the second century, " prophets " went from one church to another to encourage the Christians. They were continuing the itinerate life of the Apostle. An old writing from those times called the " Doctrine of the Apostles " shows us the signs by which we can know a false prophet, and it always comes back to the lack of disinterestedness in his conduct.

" If the prophet passes by help him as much as you can; he will stay with you for only two or three days, as necessary. Make sure that he is not idle if he stays any longer.

If he will not act thus, he is making a business of Christ—beware of such men. "

Another rule: " Every prophet demanding a table in the Spirit (i. e., commanding in the name of the Holy Spirit that a good meal be prepared for the poor) shall not eat of it; otherwise he is a false prophet. "

Our real detachment is the test of our sincerity.

Sincerity has a place of honor in our generation. Our young people want no more nonsense, and they are right. It is up to us to put our lives in harmony with our principles.

Remember these words of a peasant to St. Francis: " Be very careful to be as holy as everyone thinks you are, for the people have deep faith in you. "

Now the Apostles are settled in a house. From there their influence radiates in the village or city. They go from house to house.

For this " house to house campaign, " as we would say nowadays, the procedure was as follows. First, on entering, comes the Jewish salutation: " Peace be with you. " You recognize the salaam of which we spoke previously. This greeting is trite only in appearance; given with an apostolic and Christian spirit, it evokes that peace which the Jews had always wished each other without quite knowing what they were doing.

Now we know. This greeting of peace asks that this house where we arrive might receive the peace come down upon earth with Christ. The greeting is a beginning of the Gospel message.

And this apostolic wish is always effective. Since it springs from faith, it brings with it the gift of God. At the moment when it is invoked, peace—the gift of heaven—comes down to earth.

This grace is so productive, so active, that if a house is not worthy of it, it comes back upon the Apostle. No grace is lost. Prayer and the word of God infallibly produce their effect.

After this greeting comes the message, in its consecrated formula: " The Kingdom of God is at hand. " Then they tell of the miracles that God is working at this moment by the hands of Jesus of Nazareth : the dead rise, the lame walk, the blind see, and the poor have the good news of salvation preached to them.

The cities which refuse the message of peace " will be treated more severely, on the day of judgement, than Sodom and Gomorrah. " (*Matt.* 10: 15). Notice how the tone changes. The perspective rises to the perfection of the last judgement.

This is the terrible gravity of our apostolic mission. The grace we bear is discriminating. As one accepts it or rejects it he is saved or damned.

We are playing an active role in the drama which stretches out to the last judgement. We save souls and we damn them. It would be better for those who are damned if they had never met us.

It should make us tremble to accept such a responsibility in the apostolic life. Only one thought can calm us: if we are true apostles, no one will be able to accuse us of having played with their salvation, and the souls we shall have saved will be our crown on the day of the glorious return of our Lord.

6

The message of peace

We are wise not to resist the call of God and to "risk" the salvation of souls, for like our Lord and the Apostles, we bring to the world the greatest good.

Before the two wars one might not have known what Peace was. Now we know what the word means.

Or do we?

One day at the start of the last war, I asked a simple fellow what he understood by peace. For him it was "going to the movies and buying bananas." Without knowing it he was paraphrasing the famous saying, "Panem et circenses." The Romans cried for bread and games. This is the peace of the world, peace in the free enjoyment of earthly goods. I have never felt as I did that day the abyss which separates our Christian conceptions from those of the world.

Our peace is not that of the world. " I give you my peace, " said our Lord, " but not as the world gives peace. "

Our peace was caroled by the angels: " Glory to God! And on earth, peace to men whom He loves. " To God belong glory and the reign; to men, that peace which comes from their submission to the Kingdom of God. Our peace, as St. Paul will teach us, is the fruit of the Holy Spirit in us, justice and joy. Holiness or justice, peace and joy, are different words to express the same spiritual reality. This essential reality is our sharing in the Kingdom of God, the triumph of God in us. " May the peace of Christ triumph in your hearts! " (*Col.* 3: 15)

We are all looking for peace. Men of the world seek it on the surface of things. They want to establish it by reason or by force, the two powers of the natural order at man's disposition. And so war breaks out to see which of the two will give us peace.

The secret is to go deep into one's heart, to rely upon the presence of God. He who rests in God is safe. " God is my rock. "

Christianity (our apostolate, for its only purpose is to offer Christianity to the world) is the message of peace.

Relying on God, we shall look with calm

and sympathy upon the efforts of men and their governments to assure peace. Are these governments worthy to bring peace? Can the peace of the world be separated from the peace of God?

With all our strength we, too, desire human peace, for it can end in divine peace. It seems so much more and better capable of adapting itself to the peace of God than war. In the liturgy we ask for peace and tranquillity for the Church, safety for kingdoms and things of the world.

But just the same we know that we can remain in the peace of the Kingdom of God if that other peace escapes us.

True peace has really been given by our Lord and the Apostles, in the measure in which the world is willing to accept it.

The saints have continued *the mission of peace*. St. Francis took up the Gospel again literally as he continued the salutation of the Apostles. " The Lord, " he said, " has taught me the greeting we should use: may the Lord give you his peace. "

One day the Saint was traveling with one of his first brothers, who greeted the men and women on the road and those he saw at work in the fields with the cry, " The Lord give you his peace! "

The people had never heard religious greet them like this, and they were amazed. There were even some who became angry—" What are you after with that greeting? "

Then the brother was ashamed of his greeting, and asked the Saint to let him use another. Blessed Francis told him, " Let them talk, for they do not understand the things of God. "

The work of Christian preaching, confession and the Christian life always give the same peace through the acceptance of the reign of God.

One day St. Bernardine was preaching to the people of Sienna on peace. And God knows that they wanted peace in the strife-torn towns of Italy. " Women, do you want peace? Yes! Then give up your vanity, your rich clothing, your luxury. Stop making the churches into theaters for your flirting and your immodesty. Have a little more of the fear of God than you do now.

" All of you, citizens of Sienna, do you want peace? Yes! Then shed the sins which cover you; call back the banished; stop evil from being committed; curb usury. Oh, do what I tell you! Never try to shackle the Church's liberty, for when you rise against her you rise against Christ; and since he is more powerful than you are, you will reap only his displeasure, and will come to naught. "

What is done in the confessional, if peace is not given to consciences, returning them to peace with God, with neighbor and with self? It is not just a question of solving complex cases, but of revealing souls to themselves, forcing them to know themselves and find peace again by entering into themselves.

" Even before one came near, Father Vianney saw the kind of soul before him. From the moment you entered his presence— you could hide nothing from him. You could almost say that he entered the conscience of his penitents with more frankness and a better memory than they, and he made use of both frankness and memory. If you hid in the crowd, he walked through the crowd looking for you. It seemed as if he held a thousand invisible threads in his hands, attaching each one present to himself. He had only to pull on the right thread at the right time. " (Ghéon)

An old peasant, Mr. Rochette, had brought his wife and sick son to Ars. The Curé called him, but he did not answer. Once. Twice. At the third time, for fear of appearing too impolite, the peasant accompanied him behind the altar. " After all, " he said to himself, " he won't eat me! "

Father Vianney pointed to the confessional.

" I don't feel like it, " answered the peasant.

" That doesn't make any difference. Begin. "

The Curé began for him by reminding him first of all of certain faults he had forgotten. Rochette did not go back; he needed only continue.

And here is a penitent who analyzes herself. Her picture seems quite true to life.

" I was disturbed by a spiritual distress which was indirectly connected with my vocation but I hesitated to mention it (to Father Vianney). I found it difficult to explain myself. I was afraid that he would not understand me and thus give a decision which could trouble me for the rest of my life. I had more confidence in him than in anyone else on earth. I felt that no one could say anything to destroy the impression of his words. Since this matter did not concern the integrity of the confession, I decided (though with difficulty) to remain silent.

" I cannot express how I felt, how astonished I was interiorly, when he answered what I had hidden with an exactness I would not have dared hope for even if I had explained the matter most carefully and minutely to him. "

Blessed are the peacemakers, who bring peace to consciences. They shall be called children of God.

It is not necessary to be in the pulpit to be a peacemaker, or in the confessional to call down peace with that deep faith which gives birth to peace in those we meet. All we need is peace in our hearts, for of itself peace radiates upon others. That is how St. Benedict Labre gave peace.

All day long he was only a beggar at the church door. But he said to the faithful who mounted its steps, " My son, get rid of that thought . . . my daughter, you are now undergoing a serious temptation, but God will not abandon you. " He saw the injustice of those who thought they were just, and the impurity of those who thought themselves pure. He saw the secret deceits, the hidden jealousies, the sordid affairs and the sins of the flesh consummated in the spirit. The beggar Benedict Labre, confessor without a mandate, brought about sacramental confessions more sincere than they had ever been. For the lie was his greatest enemy. And this includes the lie of appearances when souls were concerned. " Why this crucifix in your room? " would ask Benedict Labre, pointing to the sacred symbol at the bedstead of thieves or adulterers. " Why this crucifix? It is not there to judge the state of your house, your business, your conscience? "

We begin to work for peace as soon as our lives sincerely belong to God. One of the great ways of being an apostle, of spreading the fragance of Christ, is by carrying peace within us, preserving it amid the agitation of others, and making it descend upon those with whom we live. On the last day of his life, St. Francis reconciled the bishop and the mayor of Assisi by adding a strophe to the canticle of the Sun: " Praise be to Thee, my Lord, for those who give pardon. "

7

Sheep and wolves

" Behold, I am sending you out like sheep in the midst of wolves. " (Matt. 10: 16)

Our Lord sought the most violent contrast possible. Sheep and wolves: these animals are opposed in nature, habits, temperament and tendencies. Sheep are gentle and timid, wolves are cruel, bold, and evil.

To tell the truth, the comparison flatters neither the Apostles nor the world. But for the moment let us note only that our Lord predicts setbacks and opposition for his Apostles. The cities they enter will rebel against their message, and they will shake the dust of these cities from their feet.

Our Lord's tone has changed abruptly. Some commentators even point out that the images of the discourse clash and contradict each other. Before, the Apostles were sent to the lost sheep; now, sheep themselves, they are sent to the wolves. They conclude that from here on the sermon deals with the great missions which will follow Pentecost. Perhaps. But where not the Pharisees and Herodians and Priests in Galilee wolves? We must not forget that the Gospel ever meets opposition.

When we dream of a religious life without opposition, without enemies or tribulations, it is no longer the religion of our Lord. His religion always supposes *contradiction*. We must try to understand the reason for this constant struggle in which we are engaged.

God is the Holy One. Our Lord defines himself, too, as the Holy One of God. Now, holiness brings about an immediate separation —creates a chasm between God, the all Holy One, and His creature. When God revealed Himself on Mount Sinai, the whole mountain became consecrated ground. Only Moses could cross the ring of stones which marked off the inaccessible region: Moses, the man of God, who found himself carried by grace over the threshold of sanctity.

Thus, before the holiness of God, creation is torn asunder. One part humbles itself in its nothingness; it accepts the fact that God is different from itself. But one part of creation wants to cling greedily to what it is, what positive being there is in its nothingness, forgetting that this is all a free gift. It attributes its being to itself; it glories in this being.

This is the fundamental pride of the creature, this is what offends the holiness of God.

We know by faith that the most perfect spiritual creatures, the angels, were so pleased with themselves that they led the revolt against God. Men followed, making the world a band of rebels.

Our Lord has not put down the revolt. He is waiting for his glorious return to triumph once and for all, " when he will destroy every Principality and every Power and every Domination, for he must reign until he has put all his enemies under his feet. " (*I Cor.* 15: 24-25)

While awaiting his complete victory, our Lord is content to form a nucleus which recognizes right now that God is holy, willing by obedience and humility to fit into the order He has willed.

How could this fail to introduce opposition into the world, and strife and contradiction? There is too much opposition in basic concepts. The world counts on itself. It, too, is seeking peace, but it wants to get it by itself, in the abundance and security of pleasure, in the fulfilment and satisfaction of selfish ambitions. It refuses the peace of God.

Blessed are the poor, we say, the meek, the humble, the pure of heart, those who let themselves be tormented, those who imitate

God in his goodness, his mercy, his pardon. For true strength consists in the display of the spirit.

Blessed are the rich, answer the others, blessed are the strong, the proud, the sensual, those who enjoy life to the utmost. Blessed are those who impose themselves and assert themselves, those who no longer need God. How are they to be answered?

What makes our position as apostles even more dramatic is the fact that the struggle between the two parties is now *within ourselves*.

By our very nature we are a contradiction unto ourselves—by ourselves we are proud and sensual and in love with riches. Only by the Spirit of God are we made poor and mortified.

We dread real poverty, which deprives us of our comforts. We dread mortification, humiliations, silence and recollection and solitude of the heart. But by the Spirit of God we give ourselves over to what widens the paths of God.

For the world, God's final victory will come on the last day. Alas! perhaps we, too, will have to wait until our last hour for God to achieve in ourselves the work of our salvation. God is infinite patience, and his forbearance will triumph over our misery which grows weary of itself.

As travelers in a land of wolves, we must be on our guard.

"Be prudent as serpents, and guileless as doves."

The Apostles have seen serpents gliding along in the grass, silent, discreet and ever fearful. Caution is their strength.

We also are to be cautious. We are not to throw ourselves into the jaws of the wolf, brave every danger, or uselessly stir up our enemies.

When the Church was persecuted, it hid itself. It lived in the catacombs. There were certainly bold and enthusiastic Christians who desired martyrdom, and sought after it. But St. Athanasius spent his life fleeing from the persecutors. He had his hiding places in the desert of Egypt, where the anchorites were his scouts and his protectors. If necessary, he used trickery. Pursued along the Nile in a small boat, he made an abrupt about-face and came back directly towards his pursuers. "Have you seen Athanasius?—He isn't far. Row faster!"

It is better to imitate St. Athanasius, who is a great saint, and not expose ourselves to danger. We do not know just how far our virtue will support us.

Let us beware of false sheep.

" Beware of false prophets who come to you dressed as sheep, while interiorly they are ravenous wolves; by their fruits you will know them. " (*Matt.* 7: 15-16)

We should not listen to just anyone at all. At first the false prophets imitate our customs and our language, but if we associate with them we will end up by imitating them. We are living in times of moral and intellectual disorder. The kingdom of this world is presenting itself as a religion. It is borrowing our words and our acts. It wants to make us believe that its designs are like those of the Kingdom of God, or that Christians are no better than anyone else. Let us not be taken in. We must lean heavily on the Church, its priests, its doctrine, and its prudence.

" Be simple as doves. " The dove flees, but has nothing to hide. If we are unadulterated Christians (that is what simplicity means) the enemy will have no hold on us. If we do not nourish in our hearts a certain complacency for the world and if we do not mix with the wolves we have nothing to fear.

Let us be truly what we profess to be, religious men, supernatural men, faithful men.

8

Preaching the kingdom

" As you go, preach this message ' The Kingdom of Heaven is at hand! ' " (Matt. 10: 7)

As you *go*, preach. This supposes that we leave home. Now there are two ways of departing. We " really " depart. The Apostles are doing their apprenticeship: they leave their lake, their city of Capharnaum, their job; that is hard to do.

Men in religion leave their home and family. Whoever wants to devote himself to any sort of Christian work should in one way or another abandon friends or occupations.

But that is not the main departure. The *main departure* takes place when we leave ourselves, our habits and comforts, even our will. This is done by that beautiful act of faith in the incomparable value of the Kingdom of God, for which we sacrifice all.

Once we have agreed to leave, we preach the Kingdom of God by repeating what our

Lord said: " The Kingdom of God is at hand. " That is our task for souls.

Let us understand well the present situation. The Kingdom of God is as unknown now as it was in the time of our Lord.

Everyone is waiting for " something. " From the time of our Lord, people have been waiting for God's intervention. The Jews thought that God would work a miracle for his people expelling the Romans and giving victory to them, making the Holy Land into an earthly paradise, making them swim in pleasures, or even more. These same earthly joys (or almost the same tastes, for the palaces have become more delicate, and the desires more complicated) are still being waited for today. No longer from God, but from men, from the government, from a Council of Europe, from the Atomic Age: in a word, from human energy, from human organization without God. Yet let us not exaggerate. There are profound statements of certain statesmen which bow before the Providence of God; but how many negations, sometimes clear, sometimes buried in the subtleties of a materialistic life!

Our Lord preached a Kingdom of God quite different from the one the Jews were waiting for: a spiritual Kingdom, established by God in the depth of those souls which accept it.

And we, too, also preach the same Kingdom. It is equally opposed to what the men of today are awaiting. We are preaching the beauty and the power of the spiritual and the supernatural. We are rowing against the current which is sweeping humanity away.

Like the Apostles, we repeat the words of our Lord: " The Kingdom of God is at hand. " It is within the reach of every soul of good will.

We are preaching. Every good Christian preaches, each in his own way.

There are many ways of preaching. There is that of prayer and a *fervent life*. That is the best of all, for everyone can do that.

That was the manner (almost the only manner) of St. Benedict Labre. His presence radiated holiness.

That is the real way. That is more than an announcement, for the Kingdom of God is already present, with all its force of influence and communication.

Once on a feast day Father Morelli said Mass at the altar of the Annunciation in the church of St. Ignatius in Rome. He was giving out Communion; after the first row, he was going back to the Epistle side to satisfy the devotion of other faithful who were coming up, when he stopped, " overcome by a feeling of admiration, amazement and tenderness that words could never express. " Before him knelt a poor man waiting for Communion. It was Benedict, his whole body as repulsive as his clothing. Father Morelli stood as if stunned. As he gave him the Sacred Host, after saying the words " Corpus Domini nostri Jesu Christi, " he stopped for a moment, " carried away by a sudden feeling of piety and consolation which he could no longer control. " He had to force himself to dominate this emotion and finish the liturgical words so that he could continue distributing the Holy Eucharist to the people. He could not forget this communicant; he finished Mass filled with a holy feeling of peace and joy, moved almost to tears. The picture was constantly before him of that poor man kneeling waiting for the Host.

Another priest, Father Balducci, began his Mass with an " Introibo ad altare Dei " such as he had never said before. " The words which he normally said mechanically left his spirit in all their fullness of youth and purity. " This priest experienced an intense desire to be rid of all sin.

He goes on with Mass, wrapped in fervor, as if some power were lifting him up to heaven. Then he saw Benedict, a heap of rags, and he knew by a divine intuition that this was the source of that mighty force.

One can also preach by *example*. This is how the first Franciscans preached, by the example of their evangelical lives. They were obviously poor, amid all those (even church-men) who ran after honors and riches, and in this poverty they revealed the joy of heaven. That is the most beautiful of sermons.

We preach in vain when we do not give good example. And when we have given good example, the sermon is finished.

When one is holy and gives good example, then he can preach *in words*, the third way. Use few words, the fewest possible, but words coming from a holy soul, words directly inspired by God. A year or two before his death St. Francis enjoyed a period of renewed health.

He felt a rebirth of strength and energy. It seemed as if his youth was coming back and he was beginning his life again. " Let us begin to serve God, " he said, " For until now we have done nothing. " He made great plans; he wanted to return to the simplicity of his earlier days. He wanted to consecrate himself again to the service of lepers, yet go to pray in solitude, where, as Celano says, there would no longer be anything between God and himself to separate them except the walls of his flesh. But he also wanted to work again to save souls and unite them more closely to God.

This latter plan prevailed. He found enough strength to return to his apostolic travels. He could no longer go on foot, so he mounted a little donkey and began to criss-cross the countryside. The people welcomed him like a heavenly vision: he seemed so pale, almost transfigured. At Saint Verecundus, for example, where he was known, the local peasants surrounded him. "Where are you going like that, Brother Francis? Stay with us. The countryside is full of wolves. They will jump on your donkey, and even attack you." "No, my children," replied Francis, "I have never hurt brother wolf, and he would not have the courage to eat my donkey. Good-bye; serve the Lord well." Elsewhere, as here, the sick old man could only say a few words, but these words were always full of fire. They went straight to the soul and gave new life, as in days gone by.

The holier the life, the more effective the words . . . .

Anyone can preach, "Man must humble himself, despise himself, pray at the foot of the cross, trust in the goodness of God, and wait for what happens with confidence." But when Benedict Labre said these very simple words they went to the heart.

We must also preach by fulfilling the duties of our position in life. No matter what the post entrusted to us, it can furnish us with the occasion of a live sermon. I am thinking especially of those who have the difficult (yet so beautiful) task of forming the souls of the little ones by elementary education.

If you teach reading, by this very lesson you preach. You tell the children, " Lift up your eyes. Do not lose yourselves in matter, for there is more than matter. " You help them to climb up one step in the direction of the Kingdom of God: it is like reading a musical score on which are written praises to God. Our intelligence is given to us for that.

Trust your job; love it. It is wonderful to form and build intelligences for God.

When you teach, keep in mind this noble goal. When you teach spelling, pray that this skill might lead to the Kingdom of God. If you pray, through the power of your prayer the child will later read good books, perhaps lives of the saints, instead of novels.

You must work hard yourself, and teach the children to work. Intellectual effort in particular tends toward God, because the intelligence only develops fully in intensive study. It is the great heresy of modern pedagogy to have made a game out of what should be work, an effort for the conquest of truth.

Give good example, and be devoted. The memory of those who gave him his childhood formation will be present every time the man opens a book.

Is it necessary to " preach " in class? What is most necessary is to make God felt in us. The nobleness of our life, our love of God, of sincerity and righteousness all give light from above. The land is dark: a ray of sunlight comes, changing everything, giving birth to color, then it is useless to cry that the sun exists. Such is our teaching when God gives the light.

9

" Cure the sick,
cast out devils "

St. Jerome asks himself why the Apostles received the gift of miracles, and his answer is something like this. " The Apostles worked miracles so that the people would not refuse to believe such ignorant men. "

Despite all my esteem for such a great Saint, I do not think that this is the true explanation. With the Apostles the Kingdom of God was established on earth. This was a conquest, a first victory. The Kingdom of God is made for the soul, but it is so mighty that it shines even in the body. When the devil established his kingdom by man's sin, destroying the Kingdom of God, illness and death were set up as trophies of his victory, perpetual monuments to his glory. Even today the miseries of humanity continue to proclaim the effects of original sin and every other sin that followed. If men were not sensual and proud, would we have known the cataclysms of these wars? Are not the concentration camps and such excesses of cruelty like the stamp of sin and the signature of Satan?

When the German armies reached the forest of Compiègne in their offensive of 1940, their first act was to destroy the monument commemorating the armistice of 1918, putting one up in its place telling of their own victory. And in the same way, because the devil marked his victory with sickness and death, the victory of God is commemorated by the miraculous destruction of sickness and death. At the beginning of the Gospel miracles were the visible manifestations of the victory of life and of the reestablishment of the Kingdom of God over souls, like the signature of God upon his work.

Thus, miracles are a *privilege*. But there is a big difference between the way our Lord performed miracles and the way the Apostles did them. Our Lord commands. He does not pray for miracles, he commands. " Power " goes out from him, says the Gospel. His sacred body is like a reservoir of spiritual force which cures bodies. Remember the details of the healing of the woman with the hemorrhage.

But our Lord reproaches the Apostles for not having enough faith. If they had faith as big as a mustard seed they would say to this mountain: " Throw yourself into the sea. " They have a sort of " ordinary power " to do miracles, but because they are still men, they should have faith, pray and fast. When the saints accomplish the Kingdom of God in themselves, they share in the power of the Apostles, though to a lesser degree. If we do not work miracles we should attribute it to our lack of faith and the atmosphere of sin which surrounds us.

The sick throw themselves on our Lord like a band of robbers. They crowd around him, pushing from all sides to touch him . . . just the hem of his cloak. The sick are lowered through the roofs, they are cast at his feet. As soon as they hear that he has come to a town, these pitiable processions issue forth from all the surrounding villages. Paralytics are carried on stretchers, the blind are led by the hand. Mothers hold feverish children in their arms, epileptics dance the St. Vitus dance in the midst of the crowd. The deaf-mutes run ahead to arrive first, and the lepers close the procession at a respectful distance. . . .

The Twelve shared in the privilege of our Lord, as some great saints at times did after them.

With or without the gift or miracles, the sick have remained our charge, our legacy, and to be sure that we do not deny our heritage our Lord has identified himself with them. We cannot pass by indifferently: he is that sick man. "Come, blessed of my Father, take possession of the Kingdom, for I was hungry and you gave me to eat; I was a stranger and you took me in, naked and you clothed me, sick and you visited me.—Lord, when did we visit you?—Amen, I say to you, whatever you did to one of these, you did to me."

Should we ask our Lord on that day: "Why did we not do more miracles?" he would answer, "You have *My Charity*. That is the greatest miracle of all."

"Cast out evil spirits." (*Matt.* 10: 8)

The *evil spirits* have a place apart. They are natural enemies of the Kingdom of God; they are the leaders of the kingdom of this world and the guides of the wolf pack. Our Lord's miracles also set them apart. Our Lord does not put up with them. As soon as he appears, the evil spirits flee. And this power of his he gives to his Apostles. Christians, who accept the Kingdom of God, are freed of them; we no longer fear them.

But for the moment our Lord did not wish a complete victory. That victory, the annihilation of the evil spirits, is for his glorious return. Only then will they be " annihilated. " In the meantime they are vanquished but remain powerful. They defend themselves bitterly disputing the power of the world with God. They still rule part of the world for they bring about the collusion of evil wills. They take the lead in the movement of opposition to the Kingdom of God.

As soon as men give in to them and refuse to accept the Kingdom of God, the evil spirits find a home, a very comfortable home. They see themselves in the world's pride. There is some sort of attraction between the world, material civilization, matter and the devil. The devil is at home in matter and in the anti-Christian forms which sometimes clothe this world's civilization.

When our Lord triumphed by his death and resurrection, the ancient pagan cults, the science of those days and their political might all banded together against his religion. It was like the devil's last stand to keep his tyranny unbroken.

St. Paul tells us that the evil spirits were behind idolatry. They hid behind the statues of the gods.

They were also behind immorality, and they were defending their reign.

They were behind power and riches, which so often serve as a screen for immorality.

They were behind the Roman Emperors especially the "patrons of the world," as Tertullian said. The Emperors were their lieutenants, and when a man adored them Satan triumphed.

When the Roman Empire was converted, the evil spirits appeared to loose their main stronghold. Do you think that they just faded away? They chuckled gleefully, for they knew well that those pagans who were converted *en masse* would be Christians in name only. St. Augustine and the great bishops of those times had to thunder against the pagan customs of their faithful.

In other words, the evil spirits have made a retreat. They show themselves less, they triumph less obviously; but they continue to reign. Their fury against the saints shows it.

Perhaps the story of St. Anthony's temptations in the desert is partly legend. But still, there is a profound truth here: the anchorites withdrew into the desert to meet the devil. When the supernatural world reveals itself to us in sanctity, it presents its two extremes, God and Satan.

The devil is not very interested in ordinary Christians. The saint, however, is choice game, whom he hunts relentlessly, exactly because he is so difficult to capture.

For ordinary souls the devil does not expend much imagination. A slight movement of pride, a seductive image, the caress against his cupidity, and the soul goes tumbling down the slope at whose bottom the prodigal son is tending his swine.

The saint is different. His armor of grace and prayer and penance and faith protects him. But the devil remembers his battles with the archangel St. Michael. He loves a fight, and to make a great servant of God fall is a success that shines in the annals of hell. He works unceasingly. He has found an opponent worthy of himself.

And so the anchorites struggled in the desert and St. Benedict in his monasteries. St. Francis met the devil in the hermitage of the Carceri and in the tower of a wealthy Roman estate which he used as a refuge. During a chapter meeting God once let him know that Satan, alarmed at the fervor of the order, had assembled thousands of devils, but not for a frontal attack on the Friars Minor. They planned to use trickery, and by bringing many noble and wise and rich men into the order, so to destroy its humility.

You know how the devil raged against the holy Curé of Ars. He tempted him to

97

the depths of his soul. Failing to make him
doubt the legitimacy of his unusual path, he
attacked his body. For thirty-five years the
" grappin " tormented the holy Curé to keep
him from praying, to ruin his sleep, and thus
to lessen that overwhelming apostolic activity.
And also to take revenge, basely, as the devil
knows how to do. The Saint's nights were
tormented. Rats chewed the curtains of his
bed, scratching and gnawing, and the good
Curé's pitchfork could do nothing about it.
Tremendous blows on the front door echoed
through the house; the bed curtains flapped.
The devil overturned tables and chairs,
hammered, sawed, planed the floor all the
night long. He imitated a policeman's
footsteps on the stairs, he shouted outside
like an army of Cossacks, he disputed and
discussed. Three years before the death of
the Curé, he finally set his bed on fire—to
the great joy of this holy man, who could
then say that the poorest of his parishoners
had a bed and he had none. The Saint finally
got used to all these infernal vexations: " The
grappin and I, " he would say, " are almost
friends. "

The record has been preserved of
a conversation between St. Vianney and
a possessed woman, which took place on the
afternoon of January 23, 1840 in the chapel
of St. John the Baptist, in the presence of

eight witnesses. The devil speaks with this woman's mouth, setting out all his grievances against the priest: " Ugly black toad, how you make me suffer... We are waging war on each other... But despite your efforts, sometimes you still work for me... Why do you make your penitents' examination of conscience? Could it be that the one I made for them isn't enough? You want to go away in solitude. Why don't you? Why do you get up so early? You are disobeying Purple Robe—he told you to take care of yourself. Why do you preach so simply?... People think you are stupid. Why don't you preach big, like in the cities? Ah, how I love those grand sermons that don't bother anyone, just letting the people live as they like and do what they want...."

Another possessed person told the Saint: " If there were three like you on earth, my kingdom would be destroyed. You have stolen more than eighty thousand souls from me..."

We can clearly see the powerless raging of the devil against the saints.

Today the devil continues to hide himself and his intentions.

There is no longer idol worship as in the times of the persecutions. But who knows? There are still temples built to riches and others to luxury and still others to pride.

Emperor worship is not at all dead. Don't you think that the devil might be behind these façades?

There are still terrible struggles against the Church, and bloody persecutions. Do you think that the devil exists for nothing? He will reappear at the end of time, when there will be a sort of incarnation of Satan in the Antichrist. Is he idle while he waits?

Our missionaries tell stories. . . . Father de Tonquedec, exorcist of the diocese of Paris, is sure that he, too, has crossed the devil's path.

We see the steady movement of civilization as it is drawn toward materialism. We see all the formulas for dechristianization invented—free thought, communism, the dictator cults, the cults of Progress, of " modern life, " of man's rule over the material world—and we see that it all comes down to the same thing. Then are we not forced to believe that there is someone holding the strings of the marionettes which dance across the world's stage?

Part two

GOD'S PROMISES

Behold, I am sending you out like sheep in the midst of wolves. Be therefore wise as serpents and simple as doves. But beware of men; for they will deliver you to councils, and scourge you in their synagogues. Then you will be led before governors and kings to give testimony before them and before the pagans. When they hand you over, do not be anxious about how you will speak or what you will say: it will be given to you in that hour what you are to say. For it is not you who speak but the Spirit of your Father who is speaking in you. And brother will hand over brother to death, and the father his child; children will rise up against their parents and will put them to death. And you will be for all an object of hatred, because of my name; but he who will persevere until the end will be saved. And when they will persecute you in this city flee into another. Amen, I say to you, you will not have traveled through all the cities of Israel before the Son of Man comes. The disciple is not above his teacher, nor the servant above his master. It is enough for the disciple to become like his teacher, and the servant like his master. If they have called the goodman of the house Beelzebub, how much more them of his household? Do not fear those who hate you. Everything that is concealed will be revealed, and everything hidden will be made known. What I tell you in darkness, say in the light; what you hear in the ear, preach from the housetops. Do not fear those who kill the body, but cannot kill the soul. Rather fear him who can destroy soul and body in hell. Are not two sparrows sold for a farthing? And not one of them falls to earth without the permission of our Father. As for you, even the hairs of your head are all numbered. So do not be afraid: you are worth much more than many sparrows. Who will have borne witness to me before men, I will proclaim him before my Father in heaven. But he who will deny me before men, I will also deny him before my Father who is in heaven. Do not think that I have come to cast peace upon the earth. I have not come to cast peace, but the sword. I have come to separate a man from his father, a daughter from her mother, the daughter-in-law from her mother-in-law. A man's enemies will be the people of his own house. He who loves his father or his mother more than me, is not worthy of me; and he who loves his son and his daughter more than me, is not worthy of me. He who does not take up his cross to follow me, is not worthy of me. He who finds his life, loses it, and he who loses his life because of me, finds it. He who receives you, receives me, and he who receives me, receives him who sent me. He who receives a prophet because he is a prophet, will receive a prophet's reward; and he who receives a just man in the name of a just man, will receive a just man's reward. And who will give a cup of cold water to one of these least of my disciples, because he is a disciple, will not lose his reward.

Matthew 10: 16-42

10

Persecution

The enmity between sheep and wolves ends ordinarily in persecution. It is the nature of wolves to ravage and tear and persecute; it is natural for sheep to let themselves be sheared and to be eaten.

The law must come true.

Our Lord gave *the law*. He saw his Apostles in the Jewish world, and then in the world of the Gentiles.

We are told that these persecutions did not happen in the very first mission of the Apostles. But is it so sure? When the Apostles announced the Kingdom of God, would the Jewish authorities living before Christ's death have remained idle? " Beware of men; for they will deliver you to councils, and scourge you in their synagogues. Then (later, when you will be used to these first humiliations) you will be led before governors and kings (here we are in Roman territory) to give testimony before them and before the pagans ... " (*Matt.* 10: 17-18)

Then our Lord describes the situation of the Christians. " Brother will hand over brother to death, and the father his child; children will rise up against their parents and will put them to death,—and you will be for all an object of hatred, because of my name.—But he who will persevere until the end will be saved. " (*Matt.* 10: 21-22)

One might be reading a chapter from the history of the persecutions. Tertullian needs only to take up this text word for word to draw from it one of his most dramatic effects. " Many put this hatred above their own interests. They prefer to sacrifice their own advantages, so long as they are rid of the object of their hatred. A husband, who is not jealous, banishes his chaste wife. A patient father expels from his home a respectful son. A gentle master drives away an obedient slave. No personal interest is above the hatred of the Christians. "

You know what went on when real persecutions came—heroism and sanctity and wonderful interventions of God; but there were shadows too, human weakness and compromises. We remember only the martyrs, and that is how it should be. The little individual cowardices are wiped out and ransomed by the enthusiasm of victory.

Tertullian explains the underlying cause of the persecutions, and here we find familiar ideas. " The (persecuted) Christians do not complain, because they are not surprised at their lot. The Church knows that she is a stranger here below, and that amidst strangers one easily finds enemies. Her headquarters, her homeland, her hope, her riches and her dignities are elsewhere. " Persecution, for a Christian, is in the order of the day.

But is Tertullian exaggerating? Sometimes he does. Yet listen to Augustine, a great saint and a great bishop, as he gives his marvelous definition of our Christian status. " Until the end of time, " he says, " she (the Church) proceeds across the earth like a pilgrim in a foreign land, buffeted between the persecutions of the world and the delights of divine love. "—Nothing else.

It is not surprising that the Church loves her martyrs, her witnesses. She sees herself in them. It is in her nature to have martyrs. Apostle, martyr, saint—it is the same thing in the canon of the Mass.

The Church's nature is to have martyrs— and so to be persecuted—as her nature is to be a stranger, a foreigner. In a world which is so often hostile, she is the herald of a foreign and invisible presence.

And if such is the Church's nature, the Apostle's role is to be persecuted. They are going to drive the wolf back into his lair, and so they must receive the first blows.

That is how to see things. " You shall be sheep among wolves. " In this statement of our Lord the first Christians read a law of the apostolate.

Obviously, the persecutions were more bitter at the beginning of the Church. " The world " was making its resistance; the devil was savagely defending his property.

That was a terrible time. Then the whole might of the State was turned against the Church. " During the time of those struggles which were to give birth to the martyrs, the Caesars were *necessarii saeculi*, for those against the Church needed them as their leaders. Tertullian is right when he says that the names of Emperor and Caesar which, according to the hidden designs of Providence, were names of majesty, became incompatible with the name of Christian, which was then a name of infamy. " (Bossuet)

At the end of time persecution will intensify again. The Antichrist will be there, the incarnation of Satan, and he will work such wonders as to deceive even the elect. He will sit on the throne of God, and he will persecute, with the power of man and of Satan, the faithful of those last days.

Between the beginning and the end, are we to think that persecution should cease? No. The hostility cannot cease, because of a basic antagonism which Satan continually renews.

One can live in times of calm. But even in these periods the threat is still present, and it takes courage to look it in the face.

Remember the French Revolution, not so long past. " A barn took the place of the church, a grain bin was the altar. It was forbidden to pray above a whisper. The priest was risking the scaffold and the faithful the galley. In those days it was worth the trouble to be a Christian. " (Ghéon)

Think of the dangers which hung above us, not too long ago.

Think of the dangers which hang above our brother Christians at this very moment in some lands. Distant thunder warns of an approaching storm.

Perhaps in a hundred years people will be surprised at our lack of foresight. God is asking of us to be Christians through and through, for one needs much faith and courage

113

to remain Christian in times of persecution. " Only he who perseveres until the end will be saved. "

Let us get used to the idea that we might be persecuted. We have made a treaty with the world, but the world is in the act of ripping it up. Who knows in what direction the world is moving today?

Since the normal state of the Church is persecution, are we to resolve to be martyrs?

Let us beware of facile enthusiasm. In his autobiography, Blessed Raymond Lulle (13th century) tells that after a vision of Christ crucified, when he had left the world, his wife and his fortune, he made these three resolutions:

1. To die in the conversion of the infidels;

2. To write a book refuting the false religions;

3. To have monasteries founded to teach foreing languages.

He arrived at Genoa to embark for the land of the Saracens. The rumor quickly spread through Genoa that Raymond was there to set out for the land of the Saracens to convert them, if possible, to the faith of Christ. The people were very edified, and hoped that God would work through him some remarkable good amongst the Saracens. For the Genoans had heard that after his conversion to a life of penance, Raymond had received on a mountain a certain holy knowledge for the conversion of the infidels. But if the Lord had so favored Raymond, to the great joy of the people, now he began to test him with a very serious temptation. In fact, when the ship and all the rest were ready to leave, when even his books and everything he needed were aboard, he was seized with the idea that if he went to the Saracens he would be immediately put to death, or at least imprisoned for life. So fearing for his life, like the apostle St. Peter in our Lord's passion, he forgot his resolution to die for Christ while converting the infidels. He stayed in Genoa, held there by a cowardly fear.... The ship left without him. When the ship left, he understood that he was giving great scandal to the people, and finally he fell into despair, believing that for such a sin God would condemn him. He was so heartbroken that he was seized with fever, and became very seriously ill.

Another vision later revealed to him that he should become a Friar Minor if he wished to save his soul. And he died a martyr, no longer by resolution, but by the grace of God.

II

The holy spirit

" *When they hand you over, do not be anxious about how you will speak or what you will say: it will be given to you in that hour what you are to say. For it is not you who speak, but the Spirit of your Father who is speaking in you.* "
(Matt. 10: 19-20)

This time there is no room for doubt. Our Lord is looking to the future, when the Apostles after Pentecost will bear witness with the Holy Spirit.

Until now, we have only heard of two actors in the struggle that rages around us, the sheep and the wolf. The battle did not seem fair. We were beaten even before the fight began, but here we stand, victorious. We have strength, more powerful than the world's, because the Holy Spirit is with us.

And so, in the midst of persecution intervenes something which forces the issue— the Holy Spirit. He is the Spirit of our Father, his power, his light, his wisdom; for the Spirit is all that.

We are relying on the Holy Spirit. There is nothing to fear.

This is the first time our Lord promises the Holy Spirit. He will renew his promise in other ways, but the role of the Spirit appears here as the most necessary and essential. He is the Paraclete, the lawyer for the defense.

Let us realize the situation of the first Apostles and the first Christians before the hostility of the Roman world. " It is stupendous for a man accustomed to a life by the lakeshore or seated behind a tax collector's table, to be suddenly brought before kings seated on their thrones, amidst the court of officers, surrounded by their soldiers with naked swords. Here the Apostle enters, alone, bound, his head bent. He must speak, and he dares to speak. He is not even given the chance to defend himself; he is handed over for torture for disturbing the peace of the world. " (St. John Chrysostom)

These Apostles and first Christians were ordinary common folk; and we know how much, at least formerly, courtrooms and judges were feared. Yet the Christians are hauled at once into Criminal Court, accused of the most terrible crimes. The crime of sacrilege. They are atheists, for they do not recognize the gods of all. The crime of high treason— they are the anarchists of their day. They are blamed for being useless to the state, even for being the cause of the decadence of the Empire. They are outlawed.

They withstood the persecution, but to do it they needed a higher power sustaining them. The whole history of the persecution is a continuing miracle—the Holy Spirit working in the Christians, giving them wisdom and strength.

"When we read of the victories of the saints," says St. Bruno, "we often hear stories of how philosophers and wise men were put to shame by young girls and uneducated men. Who did this miracle, if not the Holy Spirit who spoke in them?"

"Our task," wrote Theophylactus, "is to bear witness; to answer with wisdom is the role of God."

The Holy Spirit gave the martyrs strength, as well. In her prison cell St. Felicita was groaning with the pains of childbirth. "What is it going to be like," asked her jailor, "when you are in the arena?" "Now it is I who suffer," was the answer, "but then another will suffer in me."

The Holy Spirit is promised particularly for persecutions, since martyrdom is the witness to our Lord *par excellence*. Thus, "You will receive the Holy Spirit, and you will be my witness." But, whether by our words, our teaching, our works of mercy, or the example of our Christian life and the fervent accomplishment of our duties of state, whenever we bear witness to Christ, we do so *in the Holy Spirit.*

We must not be afraid *to trust our Lord's promises.* The descent of the Holy Spirit upon the Apostles on the day of Pentecost is only a first realization of the great promise. It will be renewed forever in the Church, and for all Christians. Listen to how St. Peter explains what happened on Pentecost: " This is what was spoken through the prophet Joel: And it shall come to pass in the last days, says the Lord, that I will pour forth of my Spirit upon all flesh; and your sons and your daughters shall prophesy, and your young men shall see visions, and your old men shall dream dreams. And moreover upon my servants and upon my handmaids in those days will I pour forth of my Spirit, and they shall prophesy . . . " (*Acts* 2: 16-18)

There is a man who does not underrate the value of the Holy Spirit in the Christian life.

The Holy Spirit is given more especially to those who imitate the Apostles, for he is the first witness. He is the first one sent. " Behold I send you the promise of my Father. " (*Lk.* 24: 49)

He is the Paraclete, the guide and protector of apostolic travels. That is why we have no need of human equipment.

Thus the whole work of our apostolate is completely bound up in the work of the Holy Spirit in us. We are, as our Lord promised, raised to the dignity of *prophets*.

Prophets: with the *supernatural strength* which transforms us into other men. When the Spirit of God took possession of souls, they became different men.

Are not the saints' lives miraculously transformed? Sometimes they are held in this world by a thread which seems ever ready to snap. That was the case with the holy Curé of Ars. " God refused any rest for his poor body. And yet his poor body remained at its post and grimly held on. There is a mystery beneath it all. After a doctor had examined the holy Curé more than ten years before his death, he said that the way he lived, science could not explain how he remained alive! He no longer had the essentials for life, but he refused to give up his work. Sometimes, when he went to work, going up to the pulpit or down to the confessional, he was seen to become perceptibly bent; one might have said that he was emptying himself of his substance. And suddenly his task would straighten him up; grace filled him, and the priest revived the man. " (Ghéon)

If we listened to ourselves less, the power of God would transform us too. By a miracle it could give us physical strength. In any case, it would give us supernatural strength, which comes when God's power mingles so intimately with our own that we no longer know (and one should not know) if our courage is from ourselves or from God in us.

It would give us the courage to mortify ourselves, to accept and to love an austere life full of mockery and humiliations, solitude, misunderstanding and fatigue.

Prophet: with *the light of God*. Perhaps we would know things which we would not know naturally. In any case we would see things in a new light. A bit of the Gospel, a pious reflection which until now had seemed so ordinary, suddenly becomes truly new.

The truly wise man knows the formulas perfectly; he knows them so intimately that sudden flashes of light help him discover the secret laws which link things to a world more real than appearances.

Thus the science of the saints, under the light of the Spirit, makes them penetrate into the depths of the supernatural world.

There are certain conditions to fulfill to be a prophet, and to receive the strength and illuminations of the Holy Spirit.

The first is a holy life. " On that day many will say to me: ' Lord, Lord, have we not prophesied in your name? Have we not cast out devils in your name, and have we not done many miracles in your name? ' And I shall admit, ' I do not know you: be gone from me, workers of iniquity, who have not done the will of my Father who is in heaven. ' " (*Matt.* 7: 22-23)

The prophet is the man of God, he who always does His will.

And then come prayer and fasting. We must ask for the Holy Spirit, which we do in every prayer; for the Holy Spirit is not given to us without prayer. We must fast, too. A certain austerity of life is demanded, especially the spiritual fast of solitude, consenting to think only of God and to deprive ourselves of every imagination which is not of the Kingdom of God. How could the Holy Spirit reveal himself to souls full of themselves or the voices of the world, men who waste their time and their strength on the cares of the world?

We must avoid too many material preoccupations even in connection with our apostolate. In the apostolate, let us imitate Marshal Gallieni.

" When Lyautey came to Indochina under Gallieni, his commander told him to prepare the troop ships for a difficult expedition. The day before the departure, everything was ready and they had only to await the signal. Gallieni, according to his custom, was ' giving his soul a bath ', that is, he was taking a holiday from his cares by reading an English philosopher. That was his way of preparing a fresh and untrammelled spirit for the battle, so that he would be able to make a stream of exact and rapid decisions. Lyautey was worried, and his mind returned to his work. ' Is everyting taken care of? Have we forgotten anything? ' Gallieni abruptly silenced him. ' Stop it, Lyautey. There is nothing more we can do. We must give our souls a bath if we wish to be free tomorrow. ' "

Let us also stay ever free and available, so that at any moment the Holy Spirit may enlighten us and fortify us, that it may be He who bears witness.

12

God's providence

" Do not fear those who kill the body, but cannot kill the soul. Rather, fear him who can destroy soul and body in hell. Are not two sparrows sold for a farthing? And not one of them falls to earth without the permission of our Father. As for you, even the hairs of your head are all numbered. So do not be afraid: you are worth much more than many sparrows. " (Matt. 10: 28-31)

Certainly, living in the midst of dangers or persecution, it could happen that we lose our life. The life of the body, adds our Lord. And that is all that can be touched, which is not so terrible for someone who has the faith and knows the value of the soul. Everything is won if the soul is won, even when the body is lost. Everything is lost if the soul is lost.

We are tempted to act like Blessed Raymond Lulle and to " worry about our skins. " We can not escape these human weaknesses. " The spirit is willing, " said our Lord to St. Peter, " but the flesh is weak. " (*Matt*. 24: 41)

We must not listen to our imagination. God is protecting us. God protects all His apostles. The life of our body is more precious to Him than to ourselves. Let us leave the care of worrying to Him.   A special Providence looks after apostles.

People have a great deal of difficulty today over God's Providence.   They no longer accept the idea of suffering, because they have forgotten the idea of sin and the holiness of God.   They either become rebellious or take a fatalistic attitude.   During the wartime bombardments the strongest of them steadied themselves by saying, " I will only be hit when my number is up. "   The more learned spoke in Arabic: " Mektoub "—it is written.

Christians do not reason thus.   There is surely a mystery of Providence, and it is not a mystery of poverty, as if God could just barely protect us.   It is *a mystery of riches and love*.

We have a Father in heaven.   From him comes all fatherhood.   " No one is so much a father as God, " said Tertullian.   If a father takes care of his children, our Heavenly Father takes care of us.   As Christians, belonging to the Kingdom of God who is our Father, we have a right to his protection.

To think otherwise is to think as the pagans or as the Mohammedans.

Let us read again that page from the sermon on the Mount where our Lord is instructing his big children, the men from

Galilee. He raises their souls above temporal cares, showing them the true life of the children of God, who henceforth know and observe the exact proportion of things: first the Kingdom, and all other things, but in the light of the Kingdom. " Behold the birds of the air, they sow not, neither do they reap, nor gather into barns, and yet your Heavenly Father feeds them.

Are you not worth more than they?

Learn from the lilies of the fields, by observing how they grow. They neither spin nor weave, yet I say to you that Solomon, in all his glory, was never dressed as one of these.

And if God so clothes the grass of the fields, which grows today and tomorrow will be thrown into the furnace, how much more you, oh you of little faith? " (*Matt.* 4: 26, 28-30)

We must think as children of God, with confidence in Him, leaving all exaggerated preoccupations to " the rest. " One can advance in the degrees of perfection, and yet desire to have only the bare necessities for life, for the spiritual develops more readily when we are poor. If we are too poor, we can even rejoice and thank our Father, who knows well what he is doing.

If God sends us sickness, or what seems to us a misfortune, we must thank Him.

In *The Invisible Light* Monsignor Benson tells this parable. Two children were coming home from school, a little girl and her younger brother. They had stopped to play on the bridge, and the little boy was throwing pebbles into the river, to kill the fish. A far off voice that came closer: run-away horses! There was just enough room for the children to escape if they hugged the parapet . . . But an invisible hand gently pushed the little boy beneath the oncoming wheels.

A story from the life of the holy Curé of Ars can help us understand this parable. Perhaps it was its source.

" A little boy passed his days in bed, covered with sores from head to foot, without rest, without earthly hope. The Curé bent over him.

' Are you suffering a lot, my child? '

' No, ' answered the little one, ' today I do not feel yesterday's pain, and tomorrow I will not feel today's. '

' Do you want to get well? '

' No, I was bad before I got sick, and I might be bad again. I am all right like this. ' "

" Children in whom the Holy Spirit dwells, " commented Father Vianney, " put us to shame. "

Let us love the cross. It is God's gift to His friends.

For the Apostles, Providence takes another aspect besides that of a Father. It is that

of a *friend*. Our Lord himself says so, in
St. Luke's Gospel: " I say to you, my friends:
do not be afraid of those who kill the body . . . "
(12 : 4). We children of God have become
His friends, His partners in the firm " God
and Company, " His helpers. Our business
is God's business; and God takes care of it,
for He is the most responsible and the most
concerned. That is why our life is more
precious to Him than to ourselves. Nothing
will happen to us that He has not willed, for
we are in His hands. He himself is managing
the company that hired us. Our success or
our failure is His own. Our death or our
health is of prime interest to Him. Perhaps
He simply permits the poverty of other
Christians; if he gives it to us, *He wills it*.

We might sum up the attitude which our
Lord wants of us in two points:

1. Recognize the primacy of the Kingdom
of God and the supernatural. That should
be our first care, for that is what really counts;
if the supernatural is safe, all is safe. That
is why we are much happier in poverty than
in plenty, for poverty is often more useful
for our apostolate than abundance. A Belgian
country pastor, noticing that his parishoners
had to take off their wooden shoes on account
of his parlor rug, simply got rid of the rug.
We are to have the same attitude.

2. Trust that we will not lack what is necessary—and if we do not have even that, the strength of God and the grace of the Kingdom will come as compensation. Therefore we let God choose and decide which is preferable.

In this way our Lord formed the Apostles. St. Francis obviously imitated him. When the first Friars returned from Rome to Assisi after receiving the approval of their Rule they were so enthusiastic and so full of plans that they forgot food and drink and the elementary precautions for a journey. They literally took nothing for their trip. . . .

One day they were so absorbed in God that evening came before they had even thought of eating. Hunger began to make itself felt, but they could find no sign of habitation nearby. Suddenly they came upon a man carrying a loaf of bread. This man gave them bread and then disappeared.

This attention of Providence filled them with wonder, and they were comforted by it at least as much as by the bread itself. In thanksgiving they promised never to abandon poverty despite any need or opposition.

It often happens that we can no longer distinguish between a miracle (a true miracle) and a miracle of that Providence which can make such wonderful use of natural means.

St. Augustine was right when he remarked that it is just as much a miracle for wheat to grow as for loaves to be multiplied, for the wheat grows in obedience to the order God gave in creating it.

In 1825 Father Vianney spent his last cent to buy the last house in the little square of Ars. He had sent two good Christians, Catherine Lassagne and Benoîte Lardet to the Sisters of St. Joseph for a few months to form themselves in the religious life. This was the beginning of the boarding school of Ars. Father Vianney called his project " La Providence. "

As the neighboring villages sent recruits, the number of pupils rapidly increased. Soon he decided to reserve it for unfortunate girls without families. These he gathered from thirty miles around. He brought them in from the streets, girls from eight to twenty years of age. He had as many as sixty of them at one time, and they had to be housed, and clothed and warmed and fed. Abandonment to God was always the rule.

The Curé foraged, the poor religious worked, and Providence looked over this house which bore its name. When other means failed, the good pastor turned to the miraculous. One winter his supply of grain was used up, and he had begged so much already that he did not dare again. He let St. Francis Regis in on the secret, and then sent Catherine Lassagne to the rectory attic to gather up what grain was left. When she reached the top of the stairs the door would not open; she pushed, and a cascade of grain came flowing down the stairway. The attic was full to the roof. Another time there was not enough meal. The Saint said to knead what was left. The dough rose as usual, overflowing the kneading trough. That day they baked all the bread they needed.

In 1826 the good Canon Cottolengo welcomed his first patients in " the little house of Providence " at Turin. Today they are more than ten thousand, and for a century and a half only Providence has cared for this throng of unfortunates. Prayer goes up day and night in the Church of this institution for the glory of God and for His grace. One prayer is excluded, however—for the daily bread. It is up to God to take care of His children.

When we fear and when we doubt, in our poverty or our detachment, we shall hear God say to us what He said to His saints: What have you lacked up to now?

" Nothing is lacking to those who have nothing, " said the holy Curé of Ars. " Above all God demands confidence. When He alone is charged with all our interests, He comes with His goodness to aid us and to assist us. "

13

God's success

" Do not fear those who hate you.

" Everything that is concealed shall be revealed, and everything hidden shall be made known.

" What I tell you in darkness, say in the light;

What you hear in the ear, preach from the housetops. " (Matth. 10: 26-27)

Our apostolic mission is now carried out in broad daylight. At one particular moment a transformation has taken place.

Our Lord's words were mysterious. He, the Word, did not want ringing phrases. His career was humble, for he was to die . . .

His teaching and his doctrine were the seeds, but before they could grow, these seeds needed to be watered by the blood of the cross. His teaching was not to be spread abroad to the general public until the Holy Spirit would come upon them.

The Apostles' mission was to proclaim this secret publicly, in the light of the Spirit.

"Do not fear." A boldness, an enthusiasm which is not our own will lead us. The Holy Spirit will be with us.

In the context of St. Mark's Gospel, our Lord explains more clearly what he expects of his Apostles.

" Is a lamp lit to be put under the basket? Is it not to be set on the candlestick?

" For there is nothing hidden that will not be made manifest, nothing secret that will not be revealed. " (*Mark* 4: 21-22)

Then he continues with a little parable:

" The Kingdom of Heaven is like a man who casts his seed upon the ground. He sleeps and rises, night and day; the seed sprouts and grows without his knowing how. For of itself, it produces its fruit; first the blade, then the ear, then the full grain in the ear. When the fruit is there, at once he brings the sickle, because the harvest has come. " (*Mark* 4: 26-29)

The growth of the harvest is certain; because it is the work of God, the apostolate bears its fruit. That is something sure and inevitable, giving us *complete security*. By our hands the Kingdom of God grows and ripens, even if we do not know how, if we neither see nor understand.

St. Jerome shows us the lesson the Gospel teaches here: " Let the Apostles, " he says, " bear their messianic message in all confidence and boldness. " The boldness of God—that is what our Lord demands of us.

But we must never forget that the actual position of the Church places her between two extremes, the humility of the first coming of our Lord and the splendor of his " parousia. " What we call success is like a foretaste of that final glory, but with every success should be mixed a little of the humility of the beginning. The apostolate is subjected to the double pull of these extremes; humility on the one hand and success, (God's success) on the other.

We need only consider what God has done for His saints. Look at the work of St. Francis: a very humble foundation, which he wanted very humble, of Friars Minor— " Little Brothers. " He himself was only a poor, sick man who died before he was fifty, lacking in knowledge and profane eloquence, without talents . . . not even that of administrator. We know the abundant harvest which he produced.

Benedict Labre was only a poor tramp covered with vermin.

" But when the Just One dies, everything changes;

Rome enshrines his rags on high. "

As his contemporaries said, the Saint's death was " like a spiritual earthquake. "

The holy Curé of Ars was not a very gifted priest, only a village pastor. Yet he was to be the spiritual director of France.

The saints take the last place; and God, ordinarily after their death, shows that He was preparing a very high place for them. Their influence is posthumous. God takes care of the humility of the saints, or rather He applies the law of the Kingdom of God: " What is hidden shall be known, and preached from the rooftops. "

Then let us not fear. We have the strength of God in our hands. We are doing the work of God even (and especially) if humanly we do not seem to succeed.

Nor should we fear for our spiritual lives. Our spiritual life is bound to our apostolate, which cannot succeed in God without a corresponding growth in our spiritual life.

We are souls too, seeds of the Kingdom of God and of the Father's field. The field is sown with seeds and does not ripen unless they ripen. And we are not ordinary seeds—it is as if the growth of many others depended on our own.

We are therefore engaged in a life which leads normally to sanctity; but still one can advance more or less rapidly, mistake the road, or even turn back. God can do nothing when we no longer give ourselves over to His action.

In harmony with these laws of the apostolate—humility and assured success—let us take the first steps on the *path to a spiritual life* such as God wills.

The basic disposition must be humility, where the soul recognizes itself as it is, poor and essentially needy. The humble person is completely open to the gifts of God. In fact, he pleads for them, and in this act his " ego " surrenders. He has brought " the well-armed man " into his house, he counts on God, and God will never fail him. To understand better, let us contrast this with pride and selfishness. Here love of self is perverted, the will is unbending before God's will. What comes from above is refused; the action of God is scorned, or at least met with scepticism and cowardice.

From humility comes confidence in God. God is present in us, and the business of our spiritual life is an affair where only God can help us. This is not a question of building our lives according to logical, human principles. We are to work with God and impregnate our lives with His.

Certainly, it seems impossible to reach what we are striving after, the life of an angel. That is why God has given us the virtue of hope: to count on Him. Since He has invited us to live according to Him, He helps us and strengthens us. He has given us the means to fulfill our calling. Our nature has become supernatural. It has received grace which divinizes its deepest life, and the supernatural theological virtues which let us know God, love him, and dare to will what He wills.

We can count on the " ego, " which has become a " Supernatural I. " God watches over us at every moment. Not a hair falls from our head without His will.

Since wolves are naturally stronger than sheep, in us (where there are both wolves and sheep) the sheep would be defeated; but now we are able to conquer supernaturally. We can catch up with God. Our life can become supernatural and rise to Him.

This requires all the soul's strength, every bit of its supernaturalized energy. Many people imagine that it ought to take care of itself, that God owes it to us to present Himself before us the moment we deign to want Him. Because they lack the consolations of the present life, they imagine that God is going to console them and compensate them immediately. They look upon God as a charity bureau within easy reach where they can have all kinds of special joys and little spiritual consolations.

God is not like that. Holiness is an unknown land. Tickets for travel there are not sold at the ordinary ticket windows. Bravely, courageously let yourself be dispossessed, exiled, cast adrift in the sea. Then God will be present.

Thus, the interior life dazzles, it does not enlighten. It is completely new, totally unexpected. We never dreamed it was like this, and because it is not what we thought, it is infinitely better. We need only give up our dreams and be brave enough to let God work, submissive enough to go through the disillusioning process of seeing our dreams fade. But then begins another life, the true life; for God is there, the true and living God, and not the idol which we had imagined.

145

14

The heroic life

" Do not think that I have come to cast peace upon the earth. I have not come to cast peace, but the sword. " (*Matt.* 10: 34)

We have rights with **God,** for God has made us solemn promises. He has promised us the Holy Spirit in the midst of our difficulties, to give us the strength and light we need. Light and strength will never be lacking, provided that we ask for them and are worthy of them.

He has promised us His fatherly Providence. God is as interested as we are in our success, and we are dear to Him. He has also promised the success of His Church.

Thus we have complete confidence in God.

But God also has rights with us. He had a definite idea when He created us. He conceives us in one specific pattern, which is greater than that of the ordinary Christian.

The pattern of the apostle is modelled on Jesus and his saints.

" I have not come to bring peace upon the earth. " Certainly, when we think of peace as ease, lack of dignity, softness, Jesus has nothing to do with such peace. " Stop picturing me, " he tells us, " with curly hair and a delicate beard and an insipid smile. I am meek and humble of heart, but like the ancient heroes—meek in friendship and a lion in battle. I am the Father of the prodigal son, and sometimes I go too far; but I am also the severe and unbending Master. Go to the Apocalypse for my portrait, for I am as my well-beloved disciple, who rested on my breast, saw me: clothed in the long priestly robe and girded with the golden cincture of kings, with burning eyes and a voice like the roaring of angry waters as I cast the two-edged sword upon the earth. "

According to the pattern, the saints are *strong*. Let us look once again at the three saints who have inspired these pages.

St. Francis . . . long believed to be nothing but mild, thanks to certain historians—until the day when his footsteps are followed in his little mountain hermitages. A day and a night of rain on Monte Casale teach much. There one sees Francis insensible to the bite of the icy wind and the dripping rain, spending whole nights in prayer and supplication under the " *sasso spico,* " the overhanging rock which protected him so poorly. Again we see him sharing the dish of a leper. And then there was the Lent spent on Lake Trasimeno, during which he nourished himself with half a roll—to leave to our Lord the honor of a complete fast.

We would never accuse Benedict Labre or John Marie Vianney of any lack of courage. If they were not saints, they would both have been hard working peasants, stubbornly grubbing after their profit. They remained hard and stubborn, but in the work of God.

St. Benedict Labre's mortifications had almost the strength of madness, with his vermin, the sores on his knees (and he spent hours on his knees), his weakness and his lifetime of prayer. He prayed constantly. On the street he could be seen with his hands folded, his eyes lowered, as recollected as in church.

Francis and Benedict Labre killed themselves. That is the privilege of heroes. The heroes of Homer did not die in bed, but in battle; the saints kill themselves. That is permitted, when one is holy.

Of our three models, only the holy Curé of Ars knew old age. Yet this is not exactly due to a lack of mortification, nor because he had accepted a life of ease or fled from work. After describing one of his days, we dare not believe that. He worked at least twenty hours a day, of which he spent fifteen or sixteen, and sometimes more, in the confessional.

He could not deprive himself completely of food, of course. In the morning, a piece of bread (when he thought of it), at noon and night one or two cold potatoes. (He had a week's supply cooked in an old kettle). Sometimes a third potato, but only " for the pleasure of it. "

He had tried to live on only sorrel, (" but I couldn't do it, " he confided). In Lent he would fast for three days at a time as penance.

We shall say nothing of his bloody whip, his bed, his sleep. And this is a man like us, not a saint of long ago. We are almost his contemporaries.

Yes, he did reach old age.

" He seemed fixed in old age. His long wavy white hair had turned white more than twenty years before. One could not imagine him more wasted, more gaunt, more colorless, more diaphanous. His body gave the idea, says Father Monnin, of what the ancients called ' a shade. ' One could almost see through it. And the soul, burning in those ever deeper, ever larger eyes, illuminated the yellowed parchment of his face and hands. He was racked by a continual cough; to go down the steps he clung to the wall; he was endlessly stumbling, yet never falling. One ended up believing that he would never fall and that his soul had consented to live in this mummy.

" His way of life had not changed. He always gave sixteen or seventeen hours a day to the confessional. He still sat in the catechism pulpit near the Blessed Virgin's chapel, where he spoke with gestures and looks and tears of the great goodness of God, almost unconscious of the ever growing crowd of pilgrims. " (Ghéon)

Heroic when he himself came to earth, heroic in his portraits which are the saints, our Lord thus demands that we be heroic.

Ordinary Christians should be courageous. He spoke to all when he said " Blessed are those who suffer persecution for justice sake. " And does not the parable of the narrow path climbing painfully toward the narrow gate describe the Christian way of life?

The ordinary Christian life is not easy; the apostolic life is to be heroic. The apostle should push the pattern that far. Therefore our Lord expresses himself in military terms: " I have come to bring a sword, not peace. "

Peace is ease, the ordinary life in an easy chair, with bananas and movies. Our life shall be the life of soldiers on guard, the life of those who wear the sword and *accept the sword in their life*.

The two-edged sword pierces deeply and cuts brutally. When Alexander the Great stood facing the Gordian Knot, which promised him the empire of the world, he drew his sword and cut it.

Our Lord explains what he wants of us. " I have come to separate a man from his father, a daughter from her mother, the daughter-in-law from her mother-in-law.—It is dissension that I bring to families. " (*Matt.* 10: 35-36)

We no longer belong to our families according to the flesh, unless we transform them to our resemblance. We will quite often pass for strangers in the world. " There can no longer be affectionate confidence, " says St. Jerome, " where faith divides us. "

The bitterness can increase because it is we who have changed. We have accepted a stronger love, a love which isolates us, and the world perceives it clearly. " He who loves his father or his mother more than me, is not worthy of me; and he who loves his son and his daughter more than me, is not worthy of me. " (*Matt.* 10: 37)

We give our heart to God, and He keeps it for us. We hand it over to Him and He gives it back to us to use in our apostolic life. The friendship of the family becomes apostolic charity. It would almost be easier to think only of ourselves and renounce all love of our neighbor. God is demanding a continual struggle to purify the heart we have consecrated to the apostolate. Our time, our resources, our life, our affections all belong now to our neighbor.

Thus heroism is the companion of our whole life as apostles. It is a life of renunciation from beginning to end, and from beginning to end it is also the fulfilment of our supernatural activity, the source of faith, of hope, and of love.

15

The cross

" He *who does not take up his cross to follow me, is not worthy of me. He who finds his life, loses it, and he who loses his life because of me, finds it. "* (Matt. 10: 38-39)

We have seen executioners force those condemned to death to dig their own graves. The Romans obliged the unfortunates to be crucified to carry the stake or cross on which they would be hung. That was a refinement. Jesus carried his cross like that.

But now our Lord suggests a refinement in our devotion to his service. We must be like him. We must seek and find a cross of our own, put it on our shoulders and follow the Master. Thus are we worthy of him, on the same footing, treated like him. In the eyes of God we thus become worthy of Christ.

What will it be, this substitute cross which we freely and lovingly take upon us for the honor and the joy of resembling Jesus?

Our Lord tells us: "He who finds his life, will lose it, and he who loses his life for my sake will find it."

The Christian life, and especially the Christian life lived in the apostolate and the religious life, reaches its fulfilment in suffering. The Kingdom of God enters our lives, and from that moment we feel the need to renounce the kingdom of the world together with our ease, our pleasures and our riches. We know intuitively that in this way we will help Jesus and comfort him. He did not merit his cross, we did; and it is only just that we should claim it.

St. Benedict Labre spent long hours in prayer before the Carrying of the Cross, the picture over the main altar in the Church of St. Ignatius in Rome. He would look longingly at the cross, arms stretched out to it. "Ah," he would say, "that cross is mine, it is due to my sins. It is not right for the Just One to stoop to receive it. Lord, it does not belong on your shoulder!"

There are many forms of penance, and they have often been described. On the lowest level, one renounces all sin and forbidden pleasure. The apostle will renounce what is simply pleasure. He will identify himself with his apostolate. He will remove from his life whatever is not useful and directed to the reign of God.

St. Augustine was very scrupulous about this obligation, which he extended even to ordinary Christians. But then in those days they were not yet used to the kind of Christians who decide not to imitate Christ. " To give your attention, " he said, " to something which you should not is a sin. To willingly hear something you should not is a sin. To have a useless thought is a sin. You pray, and you think about something else, forgetting before whom you stand or kneel! "

Then there are mortifications which are a little more delicate. First of all comes the penance which we have not chosen, which God has sent us, the " penance of God. "

In its ordinary form, " this is an everyday penance, since it takes in all the fatigue and discomfort, the little sufferings and annoyances of a life which is human and laborious, hard and relatively poor, that is, an apostolic life. The weaker and more defenseless and the more drawn to repose one is, the more this ordinary penance is felt, and therefore of greater value. Thus those who cannot practice penance of their choice are also those who have the most merit in accepting the penance which God sends. In this way the equilibrium is established for them, if they are wise and generous. " (L. de Grandmaison)

Ordinary form! But in a stroke of genius and sanctity, St. Paul is to turn these ordinary mortifications into the apostolic pattern *par excellence*. Twelve years before his death, he lists his service in the life of the cross:

Scourged in the synagogues, five times

Beaten with the lectors' rods, three times

Stoned, once

Shipwrecks, three (and there is at least one more to come).

Journeys, danger from rivers, from robbers, from Jews, from pagans, in the city and in the desert, from false brothers.

Work, fatigue, vigils, hunger, thirst, fasting, cold, destitution; and that interior fever, the care of all the churches; suffering from the weakness of some, the scandal of others, their pride, their misunderstanding . . . (*II Cor.* 11: 24-29).

With such a man all our categories of ordinary and extraordinary, penance of God or penance of man, are shattered. We have before us the man " who fills up in his flesh the Passion of Christ, " the man " who carries in his body the marks of Christ. " When he removed his tunic one could see his back criss-crossed with deep scars. He had not given himself the discipline, but the lectors and the Jews had done it for him. That was enough.

" To an extraordinary degree, the penance of God consists in those evils, afflictions, infirmities, listlessnesses, weaknesses and sufferings which penetrate the body and soul in an acute, special or very prolonged manner, reducing it to a very painful state, and sometimes to a sort of agony. " (L. de Grandmaison)

The penances of man, which we inflict on ourselves, normally are added to those of God. Here we need generosity, obedience and ingenuity, and above all great simplicity and humility.

St. Bernardine of Sienna has given us some excellent advice on this subject. " Christ said: ' Take up your cross and follow me. ' And this is how we will know if the cross we take is our own: if it is bearable. This is because God hates nothing which He has made. If He wants a man to mortify himself, and if our penances are agreeable to Him, He in no way intends that we should kill ourselves . . . Thus only begin what you can honorably carry out. You plan to drink no more wine? Do not carry out your plan all at once; first ask the advice of a wise and discreet person. And if you should ask my advice, I would tell you to limit yourself to not drinking pure wine, but to drink wine diluted with water. "

Then the Saint tells what happened to him before he became a Friar Minor. " I got the idea to resolve to live like an angel and not like a man ... I would do as the holy fathers had done (in the desert): I would eat wild plants when I was hungry, and drink water when I was thirsty ... I began to cook a salad of thistles and other wild plants. I had no bread, nor salt, nor oil. I said to myself, ' Just this first time, let's begin by washing and peeling it. And then, the next time, we shall only peel it without otherwise cleaning it. When we get used to it we shall make the salad without cleaning it at all, and finally we shall eat it without even culling it. ' I invoked the blessed name of Jesus, and began with a mouthful of weeds ... In all, I drank several mouthfuls of water with one of weeds and I could not swallow it. But with that one mouthful of weeds I banished all temptation. What came later was election, and not temptation. "

Even very humble mortifications can seem hard to us. To encourage ourselves, we should look to the cross. One day while St. Angèle de Foligno was meditating before the crucifix, she heard our Lord say to her:

" You brush your hair, you comb it and perfume it and tint it, you decorate it and braid it, you toss your head in conceit and in pride ...

" And I have satisfied for you, I have borne your penance. I have suffered the cruelest pains for you. Because of the lotions, the hair-dos, the ointments which your head so proudly bears, my head, as holy as it is, was pulled in every direction, seized by the hair and the beard to the point of pulling them out, pierced with thorns, struck with a reed, all stained with blood, basely jeered at and scorned, decorated with a mocking crown . . .

" Your tongue sinned, for it had complete license for slanders and calomnies, mockeries and curses. Mine remained silent before the judges and false witnesses . . .

" Your neck sinned, your shoulders, your hands and your arms . . . Your whole body sinned, for you gave it over to the delights of sleep and rest, to pleasures of all kinds. But I was nailed to the cross, and covered with dreadful wounds . . .

" Keep me company, as long as you live, in pain and ignominy, in poverty and misunderstanding. "

The memory of our sins and all the sins of mankind will stir up our generosity, so that we shall keep Jesus company.

16

Love

The word which explains the whole apostolic life, up to and including heroism, is love. " He who loves his father or mother or brother or sister more than me is not worthy of me. " The strong friendship of a father, the tenderness of a mother, the gentle companionship of brother and sister, in fact all the apostle's friendships are claimed by Jesus.

If he wants us heroic, it is because he loves us and we love him. We could not be happy in loving him, he knows, if our love did not make us come to him.

The love of the apostle for our Lord is the love of a friend, disciple and servant. Such love, even on the natural level, is very strong. Remember Flambeau, the old soldier of Napoleon, in " L'Aiglon. " He had succeeded in slipping among the servants of the castle of Schoenbrunn, to continue to serve his Master's son. At night, as all slept in the castle, Flambeau would don his musty uniform, place Napoleon's hat on the table of the antechamber . . . and stand guard, just as in the old days. . . .

What characterizes this love is that it pushes us to *resemble* our friend and master. A disciple's ideal is to become like his master, to be treated like him, to think like him. He even takes on his master's way of doing things. " The disciple is not above his teacher, nor the servant above his master. It is enough for the disciple to become like his teacher, and the servant like his master. " (*Matt.* 10: 24-25)

Franciscan legend has piously preserved the memory of Brother Simple John. He is the one who took the broom out of St. Francis' hands and swept the church in his place. He felt bound to do everything that Francis did. When St. Francis was at prayer, in a church or elsewhere, he always wanted to see him and imitate all his actions. Whether Francis knelt or raised his hands to heaven, or spit, or gave a sigh, Brother John did the same. When he noticed this, St. Francis jokingly chided him for his simplicity. He answered, " I have promised to do whatever you do, Brother, and so I must imitate you. "

Brother John died not long afterwards, and henceforward Francis spoke of him only as Holy John.

The Lausiac History contains a similar example. A man of some sixty years, deceived by his wife, knocked at the door of St. Anthony's desert hermitage, to become a monk. After four days Anthony agreed to let him in and give him a try.

Anthony ate only every five days. For four days he had the old man braid palm leaves, then undo his work. Simple Paul was not discouraged and did not complain. The fifth day, Anthony said:

" Shall we eat a bit of bread? "

" —As you wish, Abbot! "

Anthony took a biscuit for himself and three for the old man.

" Eat another biscuit, my friend. "

" If you eat, I will, but if you don't, I won't."

" I have enough, for I am a monk. "

" I have enough too, for I also want to be a monk. "

At night, the novice chanted the psalms like Anthony.

"If you can do this every day, stay with me."

" If you ever do anything more, I don't know if I can. But what I have seen, I can do with ease. "

He persevered and became a great monk.

We shall have the same career as our Master. As he was treated we shall be treated—this shall be our joy.

In the beginning our Lord met with success. The crowds flocked after him: " No one has spoken like this man. " They were full of enthusiasm over his doctrine and his miracles. They proclaimed him prophet and Messias.

But Jesus deeply offended the Pharisees and Chief Priests. When the people, who followed him for his miracles, saw that Jesus was demanding an effort of them, they no longer walked with him. For this Messias was leaving them in their poverty, and was satisfied to proclaim " Blessed are the poor! " Our Lord's relatives did not trust him, and many of the disciples of those first days abandoned him. The final act of this drama *ended with the Cross.*

The meaning of our apostolic life will reveal itself to us little by little, and it will be based on our model. In the beginning, one might believe in these easy successes. If others have not succeeded, it is because they began badly. Truth is so simple, and charity so powerful.

Then we come face to face with reality, complicated with so much rancor and mistrust, so many errors committed. All the weight of it comes down upon our shoulders.

The first disillusionments force us to reflect. We must apply our effort at a deeper level, the level belonging to grace and prayer and the sacrifices which reach to God. The work of an apostle is not ordinary work. His whole soul is engaged in the conquest of a soul; and God is in the soul to be conquered as well as in the conquering soul.

In the end we will understand that the best part of our activity is not the external labor, but what is done in the depths of our soul. There it is as if we are the instruments of a great spiritual reality which mysteriously goes beyond us. We abandon ourselves to the mystery and let ourselves be fashioned like our Lord, even on the cross.

" The cross is the ladder to heaven, " said the holy Curé of Ars. " He who does not live the cross might well save his soul, but with great difficulty. He will be only a tiny star in the firmament, but he who shall have suffered and fought for his God will shine like the sun itself. "

For apostles the cross becomes a double ladder. The apostle must always lean the cross of others on his own.

If the resemblance with our Lord, going even to the cross, is inseparable from the lives of the saints, it is because of their love.

In 1777 an obscure French painter, André Bley, had an order for one of those paintings which the churches and monasteries of Rome were buying in series: " the Calling of Peter. " On the steps of the Piazza di Spagna a motley group of beggars offered to serve as models. The painter had found enough apostles, but still needed a Christ. He discovered " a young man with a short red beard dressed as a beggar, " though with none of the beauty taught in the art academies. Listening for once to the voice of spiritual beauty, Bley wanted to get the beggar to come to his studio to model the Christ. Model the Christ! The poor man shuddered in horror, as if he had heard some hideous proposition, bowed his head and returned to his beads. The beggar was Benedict Labre.

How can one explain that extraordinary resemblance which struck his contemporaries and which still strikes us in the rare authentic portraits we have of the Saint?

When Benedict meditated on the Passion of the Savior, he saw in ecstatic contemplation, and what he saw transformed him. St. Paul speaks to us of the interior transformation of our soul to the image of the Christ who died and rose again. In Benedict Labre the transformation was so intense it touched the lines of his face.

The more the Saint advanced in perfection, the more his exterior resemblance mirrored the divine model which he had chosen; his face became the face of the suffering Christ, an *Ecce Homo*.

Later, at the end of his life, a triumphant joy began to shine on that agonized face, as in the look of the dying Christ one can already see the dawn of the resurrection.

" This great servant of God, " says Father Temple, his friend at Loretto, " was so poor, so exhausted and at the same time so joyous, yet with a completely heavenly joy. When I watched him carefully, after becoming aware of his true spirit through our conferences, it seemed to me, all allowance being made, that I could see in him the most perfect picture of the crucifix. For he had constantly before him the divine model, whom the Father has commanded us to imitate: *Inspice et fac secundum exemplar quod tibi monstratum est*—consider and imitate the model! "

" Consider and imitate the model. " Let us remember Father Temple's words. Our love will give us both the desire and the strength to resemble our Lord.

17

The reward

" My apostle, who will have borne witness to me before men, I will proclaim him before my Father in heaven! " (Matt. 10: 32)

The glory of it! The abyss of holiness before which the angels veil their faces opens before us, in the presence of the Blessed Virgin Mary and all the saints! The world has collapsed, all its glory vanished like the mist. And the voice like roaring waters proclaims our names.

A canonization at St. Peter's in Rome is splendid, but a canonization in heaven! Then what difference do a few earthly cares make?

Witness for witness. Our apostolic life was our witness for our Lord; in humiliation, renunciation and mortification, we have borne that witness which goes as far as to identify ourselves with the Crucified. And now he who was crucified is triumphant, and he makes us share in his triumph.

The apostolate confesses our Lord before a human tribunal, but in reality the scene of earth and that of heaven are only one, and the earthly confession reechoes in the tribunal of God. In the mystery of the last judgement it has already given us a crown.

Thus the joy of victory begins here below. That is a law. Just as the confession of our apostolate echoes in heaven, the proclamation of our Lord at the last judgement already makes our human hearts tremble with joy.

The saints speak in guarded terms of the heavenly joys which overwhelm them. Each one has his own degree, but none of them, and no apostle, is deprived of joy.

There are two kinds of lives. There are those lives which have halted the work of God, where the divine current is cut off, lives turned in upon themselves, lives desolate and sterile as a desert. In this wasteland are the desert plants, substitute joys, the satisfactions of self love and loves less noble. But there are also lives where self is handed over to the work of God and its mysterious double action: the mystery of suffering and the mystery of joy.

Agnès de la Gorce entitled her biography of Benedict Labre *A Poor Man Who Found Happiness*. Benedict Labre! His is the last human heart where one would hope to find joy.

In the last weeks of his life his confessor, Father Marconi, saw him leaning on his staff between two columns near the altar of the Virgin in St. Ignatius' Church, more miserable, more disheveled than ever. " He would have been frightening, were it not for his cheerful face. "

At this time there was nothing to hinder the Saint's joy. He told Father Marconi that he had been freed of temptations; and not only temptations, but of scruples and of his last attachment to himself and to this sadness. " Benedict renounced the sorrowful feeling of unworthiness in which he was too satisfied; he tore away the clinging tatters of the old man. Having offered all to God, deprived even of his abjection, the poor man entered into that definitive joy which demanded total destitution of self; he turned a smiling face towards the host. " His joy had a superhuman radiance.

The last test is that of joy. Their last sacrifice carries the saints into perfect joy. God is already putting a scythe to the harvest; this is the beginning of glory.

In 1919 a rival of Benedict Labre, the poet Humilis (Germain Nouveau), died in the little village of Pourrières. He had fasted his last Lent, and he died two days before Easter. Albert Lopez called his biography:

The Strange Life of Humilis. It is a strange life, for his austerity is completely lacking the atmosphere of joy. And I think that, for that reason, it is not the life of a saint.

Does the apostolate procure other rewards, for example the recognition of those to whom we devote ourselves, or other human advantages?

" He who receives you, " says our Lord, " receives me, and he who receives me, receives him who sent me. He who receives a prophet because he is a prophet, will receive a prophet's reward ... He who shall give a cup of cold water to one of these least of my disciples, because he is a disciple, will not lose his reward. " (*Matt.* 10: 40-42)

Instead of speaking of our reward, our Lord thinks only of the reward of those who receive us. It is *as if we did not exist!*

Might this not be another example of our Lord's tact? He would belittle us by speaking of a human reward. It is enough for us if our apostolate brings peace and joy to others. We are paid in our own disinterestedness, for to work without reward is our great reward.

When we consider our work we have a right to ignore its gaps and imperfections, with everything that darkens and saddens and makes us feel our limitations. We are working in another's name. He is in our place, he speaks in us, he shows through us. It is he whom the people welcome in us.

Our failures are due either to ourselves or to God. If they are due to ourselves, it is not important. It just means that there is still something in us to be burned out, something human at work. Glory to God who wants to make of us a perfect instrument of His will!

Or else they are due to God. Then let us say: " *Dominus est.* " He is the Master. He judged that it was better this way, and so it *is* better, for He is God. And if we succeed, let us attribute it to Him too. " He gives the increase. " We should think of ourselves only to recall our sins.

We disappear, and everything is in order. God is in His place, and we are in our place, as creatures: we have the supreme honor and the supreme joy of " representing " God and procuring His glory.

Such is perfect joy: to be forgotten, because we represent our Lord so perfectly that one sees only the Master through the figure which we are.

This is how St. Francis describes the apostle: " In a painting of God and the holy Virgin on wood, God and the Blessed Virgin are honored; the wood and the paint take nothing to themselves. Thus the servant of God is like a painting of God in which God is honored for His goodness. He should attribute nothing to himself, because before God he is less than the wood of the painting. He is only pure nothingness, which is why he should give glory and honor to God alone, accepting for himself only shame and tribulation as long as he lives in the miseries of this life. "

It was a clear spring morning when our Lord, after instructing his Apostles, sent them out to cure the sick and announce the Kingdom of God.

The Apostles left two by two, greeting no one along the way, prudent as serpents, simple as doves, the Lord's prayer upon their lips.

Our life is a perpetual departure, in the clear morning of springtime. It is always spring for God, always morning. The Apostles are always young, and the departure is always a beginning.

* *
 *

Printed in Belgium by Desclée & Cie, Éditeurs, S. A. Tournai. 10.401